The Andrew R. Cecil Lectures on Moral Values in a Free Society

established by

The University of Texas at Dallas

Volume XII

Previous Volumes of the Andrew R. Cecil Lectures
on Moral Values in a Free Society

THE MEANING OF THE FAMILY
IN A FREE SOCIETY

The Meaning of the Family in a Free Society

ANDREW R. CECIL
MARY ANN GLENDON
MADELEINE M. KUNIN
ROSEMARY M. COLLYER
CHRISTOPHER LASCH
ROBERT W. CORRIGAN

With an Introduction by
ANDREW R. CECIL

Edited by
W. LAWSON TAITTE

The University of Texas at Dallas
1991

Library of Congress Catalog Card Number 91-065298
International Standard Book Number 0-292-75140-0

Distributed by the University of Texas Press,
Box 7819, Austin, Texas 78712

FOREWORD

The University of Texas at Dallas established the Andrew R. Cecil Lectures on Moral Values in a Free Society in 1979 in order to provide a forum for the discussion of the important issues that confront our society. Each year since, the University has invited to its campus scholars, businessmen and members of the professions, public officials, and other notable individuals so that they could share their ideas on these issues with the academic community and the general public. The Cecil Lectures have become a valued tradition not only for U.T. Dallas but for the wider community in the twelve years of their existence.

The University named this program for Dr. Andrew R. Cecil, its Distinguished Scholar in Residence. During his tenure as President of The Southwestern Legal Foundation, Dr. Cecil's innovative leadership brought that institution into the forefront of continuing legal education in the United States. When he retired from the Foundation as its Chancellor Emeritus, Dr. Cecil was asked by The University of Texas at Dallas to serve as its Distinguished Scholar in Residence, and the Cecil Lectures were instituted. In 1990, the Board of Regents of The University of Texas System established the Andrew R. Cecil Chair in Applied Ethics. It is appropriate that the Lectures and the Chair honor a man who has been concerned throughout his career with the moral foundations of our society and has stressed his belief in the dignity and worth of every individual.

The twelfth annual series of the Cecil Lectures was conducted on the University's campus on November 12 through 15, 1990. The theme of the 1990 Lectures was "The Meaning of the Family in a Free Society." On behalf of U.T. Dallas, I would like to express our gratitude to Governor Madeleine M. Kunin, to Professor Mary Ann Glendon, to Mrs. Rosemary M. Collyer, to Professor Christopher Lasch, to Dean Robert W. Corrigan, and to Dr. Cecil for their willingness to share their ideas and for the outstanding lectures that are preserved in this volume of proceedings.

U.T. Dallas also wishes to express its appreciation to all those who have helped make this program an important part of the life of the University, especially the contributors to the Lectures. Through their support these donors enable us to continue this important project and to publish the proceedings of the series, thus assuring a wide and permanent audience for the ideas the books contain.

I am confident that everyone who reads *The Meaning of the Family in a Free Society*, the Andrew R. Cecil Lectures on Moral Values in a Free Society Volume XII, will be stimulated by the ideas presented in its six essays.

ROBERT H. RUTFORD, President
The University of Texas at Dallas
March 1991

CONTENTS

INTRODUCTION

by

Andrew R. Cecil

Sir Thomas More (1478–1535), the Lord Chancellor of
England who was beheaded by Henry VIII for his firm
allegiance to the pope and for refusing to subscribe to the
Act of Supremacy and who was canonized by Pope Pius
XI in 1935, offers in his book *Utopia* the classic vision of
an ideal state where the family serves as the basic unit.
In More's imaginary state, built on faith in both a natural
order and the innate goodness of all, families are assured
of a livelihood so they can pursue their spiritual and cultural needs. At present the adjective "utopian" is often
used to describe impractical, idealistic dreams, but the
family as a social institution resting on a solid foundation
of historic values remains a very practical institution—
the fundamental social unit, rooted in human love and
cultural tradition.

The moral climate within a family and the model of
organization and behavior the family adopts depend on
religion, on customs, and on the dominant social and economic trends of the times. The Bible has illuminating
records of patriarchal families, and some anthropologists
tell us that the patriarchal period in family relations was
preceded by matriarchy. Closer to our own times, Victorian moral idealism cultivated a patriarchal family
structure based on evangelical religious practices. Within this structure, the idea of the sanctity of the home was
nurtured, with daily family prayers playing a powerful
role. The virtues of marital fidelity; of strong bonds be-

11

tween parents and children, brothers and sisters; of self-discipline, obedience, and chaste love; and of a sense of familial duty spread from individual family life into Victorian society.

The "great American experiment" also called for a society rooted in family and in religious values. It was, however, a new kind of family, differing profoundly from the patriarchal structure still dominant in Europe. The European family stressed a discipline that reflected the theological structure of Evangelicalism. The "new" American family was based not on a rigid formality in the parent-child relationship but on an equality that ensured, as Alexis de Tocqueville noted, that "every word a son addresses to his father has a tang of freedom, familiarity, and tenderness all at once, which gives an immediate impression of the new relationship prevailing in the family." (*Democracy in America*, trans. by George Lawrence, Harper & Row, 1966, p. 563.)

In this series devoted to examining *The Meaning of the Family in a Free Society*, I have tried in my lecture "Characteristic Values of Family Life: Historical Background" to survey changes in attitudes toward the family as the fundamental social unit and the assaults wrought by these changes against established beliefs in the importance of family life and the sanctity of the home—beliefs more central to the life of a democratic society than any other. Noting how the destiny of a free society is linked with the strength and vitality of the family, I discuss the destructive forces that have debilitated the institution of the family and explore how we can counteract the philosophy, all too prevalent today, that calls for escaping from the "bondage" of family life.

The virtues necessary for family life are intimately interconnected with the virtues indispensable for the survival of a free society. This interrelation was stressed by the Chinese philosopher Confucius, who about 2,500 years ago wrote:

> "The teaching of filial piety is a preparation for serving the ruler of the state; the teaching of respect to one's elder brothers is a preparation for serving all the elders of the country; and the teaching of kindness in parents is a training for ruling over the people. . . . When individual families have learned courtesy, then the whole nation has learned courtesy. When one man is greedy or avaricious, then the whole country is plunged into disorder. Such is the law of things." (*The Wisdom of Confucius*, ed. by Lin Yutang, The Modern Library, 1943, p. 146.)

Family life demands adherence to such virtues as commitment, loyalty, integrity, and authority. The same virtues form the underlying principles of a social system. What happens within the family shapes the life of a society and the concept of citizenship embodied in it.

Professor Mary Ann Glendon in her lecture "Virtue, Families, and Citizenship" examines four stereotypical assumptions about the relationship between the family and political and economic life and finds all of them wanting. Much more important, she finds, is the need to examine the role of the family in preparing citizens capable of sustaining the institutions of self-government that our forefathers bequeathed to us. In a society that seems to value liberty above all else, often at the expense of other equally important values, it would seem that only the family is able to foster and teach the communitarian virtues and attitudes that are necessary to bind a society together.

As Professor Glendon observes, our culture is making it ever more difficult for families to inculcate and to live out such values. A very real danger exists that the qualities of mind and spirit that the founders of our country knew to be essential for its preservation are not being passed on to future generations. Is there any hope that this defect can be remedied? Professor Glendon believes that both government and business can help solve this problem by recognizing the special status of families engaged in raising children and by assisting them in this task. Voluntary associations can also play an important role in forming networks of support for families endeavoring to pass on the torch of freedom and social responsibility.

Both experience and conventional wisdom confirm that parent-child interaction plays a unique and indispensable role in developing responsible citizenship. When families are not tied closely together, serious social problems arise. One of these problems confronting us is long-term care for longer-living citizens. Seeking freedom from our responsibilities toward our parents and grandparents, we warehouse them in retirement homes. Thus we silence the voice of conscience that gives us the power to distinguish between right and wrong.

Another trend we have witnessed during the last quarter century is the influx of many mothers into the labor force. This move of women out of the home and into the workplace and the growing number of single-parent families have brought about great changes in traditional family life-styles. The issue of child care has thus gained a prominent place on the national agenda. Various remedies have been suggested to enable two-earner families—who find themselves in economic situations that do not permit them to spend much time with their children—to select adequate substitute care arrangements. Among the remedies that have been proposed are a children's tax credit that would enable low-income families to pay for substitute care; reduction of the tax burden on families with children by raising the dependent exemption; taxpayer-funded day-care services; and the recent parental leave legislation, vetoed by President Bush, that would have both given workers in companies of 50 or more employees up to 12 weeks of unpaid leave without risk to their jobs and eased the burden of parents (mostly women) in simultaneously carrying out their job and parenthood responsibilities.

In her lecture entitled "American Families: How Do We Pick Up the Pieces?" Governor Madeleine M. Kunin describes the ways in which governmental policies in the State of Vermont have sought to assist families. Much of the effort has been expended in helping to make families self-supporting. Governor Kunin believes that the best way to get families off welfare rolls is to provide the education, child care, and health care that will enable parents to compete in the work force. The children of our country are one of its greatest national resources, and both business and government need to be persuaded to invest in that resource.

Governor Kunin also stresses the importance of promoting responsibility within families. Like many other states, Vermont has recently made strides in securing compliance with child-support laws so that fathers must now be held accountable for the economic well-being of their children. Governor Kunin's state has also experimented with creative programs that provide opportunities for young unwed fathers to get to know their children and form emotional bonds with them, thus fostering patterns of care and duty in more personal terms. Governor Kunin hopes that such an emphasis on the principle of responsibility will impart to our children a sense of values and of belonging.

As we have seen, the increased participation of women in the labor force has spurred a great deal of concern about the strength of the traditional family in our society and the care we give to our children. These concerns are not new ones. The Industrial Revolution, which largely removed the workplace from the home, was characterized at its beginning by a brutal contempt for human life and a reckless exploitation of women and children, who left home to work in garment factories and other industrial centers. Because of this displacement caused by technological changes, at the turn of the century, labor leaders embarked on a fight for "living wages" for the male workers that would enable them to support their families and permit married women to devote themselves to childbearing and discharging their family responsibilities.

This pattern was reversed in the 1960s, when enormous changes in the role of women in society began to occur. Women started moving into jobs previously held by men. Female employment has continued to climb and has been accompanied by a rise in the average age at which women marry, a rise in the divorce rate, and a decline in family size. According to the Bureau of Labor Statistics, women will make up more than half of the new entrants into the labor force between now and the end of the century but will account for almost two-thirds of the labor-force growth. More men than women will be leaving the labor force in the coming years because current male workers are, on average, older than female workers, and more older men than women have been covered by pension benefits, enabling them to retire earlier.

In 1960 only 34.8 percent of women were in the work force, compared to 57.8 percent in 1989; the number of female doctors in the last three decades climbed from 15,672 to 108,200, of female lawyers and judges from 7,500 to 180,000, and of female engineers from 7,404 to 174,000. All told, since the early 1970s, women have increased their participation in medicine, law, and management by 300 percent to 400 percent. The number of women in elected office at the local level has tripled since 1975. Asked to select the most important goal for the women's movement, participants in the *Time*/CNN poll rated "helping women balance work and family" as number one; second was "getting government funding for programs such as child care and maternity leave." (*Time*, December 4, 1989, pp. 82 and 86, and Special Issue, Fall 1990, p. 15.)

In 1990 a turning point took place in American history. Following Iraq's invasion of Kuwait, for the first time American husbands had to watch their wives and the mothers of their children go to war. Women made up 11 percent of the nation's 2.1 million active-duty military personnel. Parents and single mothers who volunteered for active duty were required to sign legal documents designating a guardian in case they were deployed or killed. Clearly the sacrifices demanded by women's entrance into the military, as well as into the work force, have had a great impact on family life, especially since plans for such careers have not excluded women's aspirations for marriage and children.

Rosemary M. Collyer, in her lecture "The Role of Women in the Work Force and Its Impact on Family Life," details some of the conflicts and compromises that can arise between professional careers and committed family life. She notes that there are inevitable sacrifices and hardships within a family where there is only one parent or where both parents work. She also notes that discrimination continues to exist within the work force, based on the assumption that a woman, especially a mother, may not be fully competent to do her job. It can still be very difficult for men in business, the professions, or government to accept women fully as their peers.

Rejecting the idea that working women should be divided into two categories (one for whom careers are clearly primary and another for those who try to balance career and family), Mrs. Collyer seeks ways in which all people with families can better combine their responsibilities to their work lives and to their home lives. She acknowledges that better child-care services will help in this endeavor, but she points out that wider issues are involved. Jobs must be restructured to permit parents to discharge their family responsibilities with less impairment of their working efficiency and with less danger to advancement within their careers. She notes that it will take time before a consensus for such changes develops but argues that such changes are vitally necessary.

The attention that the feminist agitation of the 1960s drew to the effort against the confinement of women's lives to housekeeping and motherhood may have given some people the wrong impression that until that decade women had been excluded from the important reform movements of the nineteenth and twentieth centuries. In fact, more than a century ago the fight for equal rights for women grew under the leadership of such courageous reformers as Lucy Stone, Susan Brownell Anthony, Elisabeth Cody Stanton, and others who struggled with all available means to promote the women's suffrage movement. The battle for women's suffrage was won in the United States in 1920 (20 years earlier than in France, 2 years later than in Great Britain and Germany).

In *The American Scene* (1906), the best of his series of topographical writings, Henry James wrote that in America only women were building a civilization and "men are not to be taken as contributing to it." In "developing and extending her wonderful conquest," the American woman commands "absolutely all of the social [life of the country]," so that "she has beguiled, she has conquered the globe." (Charles Scribner & Sons, 1946, pp. 164, 347.) Women were very active in—and often the moving spirit behind—the enactment of legislation for the protection of children and for the establishment of public services and facilities designed to promote the participation of the masses in civil life. We can safely say that numerous chapters have been written in the history of woman's role in the family and in the society in which she raises her family.

The recent expansion of the suburbs, according to Pro-

fessor Christopher Lasch in his lecture "The Sexual
Division of Labor, the Decline of Civic Culture, and the
Rise of the Suburbs," also inaugurated a new era in the
history of women and their roles in family life and the
broader life of society. Professor Lasch traces in the cultural history of our nation the contribution of the same
legion of civic volunteers that Henry James had noted
and finds that these women had an enormous impact on
American society. It was only in the move to the suburbs
after World War II that this tradition was largely lost in
the social fragmentation and spiritual alienation of suburban life. In reexamining two famous books from three
decades ago, Betty Friedan's *The Feminine Mystique*
and Paul Goodman's *Growing Up Absurd*, Professor
Lasch observes that both these writers had identified the
same malaise—the aimlessness and sterility of a life in
which breadwinners supported their families through
pointless jobs and homemakers had little sense of accomplishment because they were cut off from the larger
society.

Professor Lasch, however, believes that Friedan's suc-
cessors in the feminist movement failed to make use of
this insight. Instead of trying to find ways to integrate
home life and work life, they wholeheartedly bought into
the ethic of career advancement at the sacrifice of other
values—the very attitude that Goodman had found so destructive of the American spirit. In Professor Lasch's
view, a much more convincing critique of social structures in our country could be accomplished by seeking to
remodel the workplace around the needs of the family.

One of the most useful places to seek insight about developments in any culture is in its artistic productions.
This is especially true when we seek insights into the

relationship between family structures and a society, because literature has since ancient times reflected the life of the family and all its social ramifications. The story of Agamemnon and his daughter Iphigenia, for instance, is part of the background of two of the greatest works of Greek literature, Homer's *Iliad* and Aeschylus' *Oresteia* trilogy, and is the subject of one of Euripides' most famous dramas, which has been much translated and imitated. Throughout the history of literature, family life, with its joys and tragedies, has taken a prominent place.

Dean Robert W. Corrigan in his lecture "The Family and the Modern Theater: Representations of Change" notes that the increasing privatization and isolation of the individual family unit in the last century has had its parallel on the stage. With the "classic" first phase of modern drama—the generation of Ibsen, Strindberg, and Chekhov—the locus of dramatic action shifted from public spaces like palace and village square to the family living room. Whole new styles of acting and production had to be invented to mirror this change; the test of a fine actor was no longer his elocutionary eloquence but his emotional truth and subtlety, and the box set was invented to place onstage convincing rooms in ordinary domestic settings.

In the turn away from naturalism on the stage since the middle of the twentieth century, recent drama has had to find new forms to mirror the new structures society is creating. Dean Corrigan points out that it is impossible to predict what kinds of forms artists will create in the future—spontaneity and unpredictability are hallmarks of the creative act. But he is confident that future writers for the theater will have to take into account the enormous changes that are occurring in family life. Our society is groping with the apparent need to redefine just what family life is or should be.

In the 1990 Lectures on Moral Values in a Free Society, the theme is repeatedly stressed that there is a need for equilibrium between work and home. Both women and men try to reconcile professional challenges with family responsibilities. The trade-offs between work and family may cost a loss of promotions or a cut in pay. Such sacrifices are, however, in most cases acceptable, since there is a loud, clear voice calling for the revitalization of family values and principles that are essential to the proper functioning of family life. The proceedings of the 1990 Lectures examine these values and explain why they should be cultivated and honored in order to prevent the family from becoming a casualty of the assaults against it and against the traditional belief in its importance.

CHARACTERISTIC VALUES OF FAMILY LIFE: HISTORICAL BACKGROUND

by

Andrew R. Cecil

Andrew R. Cecil

Andrew R. Cecil is Distinguished Scholar in Residence at The University of Texas at Dallas. In February 1979 the University established in his honor the Andrew R. Cecil Lectures on Moral Values in a Free Society and invited Dr. Cecil to deliver the first series of lectures in November 1979. The first annual proceedings were published as Dr. Cecil's book The Third Way: Enlightened Capitalism and the Search for a New Social Order, *which received an enthusiastic response. He has also lectured in each subsequent series. A new book,* The Foundations of a Free Society, *was published in 1983.* Three Sources of National Strength *appeared in 1986, and* Equality, Tolerance, and Loyalty *in 1990. In 1976 the University named for Dr. Cecil the Andrew R. Cecil Auditorium, and in 1990 the University of Texas System Board of Regents established the Andrew R. Cecil Endowed Chair in Applied Ethics.*

Educated in Europe and well launched on a career as a professor and practitioner in the fields of law and economics, Dr. Cecil resumed his academic career after World War II in Lima, Peru, at the University of San Marcos. After 1949, he was associated with the Methodist church-affiliated colleges and universities in the United States until he joined The Southwestern Legal Foundation. Associated with the Foundation since 1958, Dr. Cecil helped guide its development of five educational centers that offer nationally and internationally recognized programs in advanced continuing education. Since his retirement as President of the Foundation, he serves as Chancellor Emeritus and Honorary Trustee.

Dr. Cecil is author of fifteen books on the subjects of law, economics, and religion and of more than seventy articles on these subjects and on the philosophy of religion published in periodicals and anthologies. A member of the American Society of International Law, of the American Branch of the International Law Association, and of the American Judicature Society, Dr. Cecil has served on numerous commissions for the Methodist Church and is a member of the Board of Trustees of the National Methodist Foundation for Christian Higher Education. In 1981 he was named an Honorary Rotarian.

CHARACTERISTIC VALUES
OF FAMILY LIFE:
HISTORICAL BACKGROUND

by

Andrew R. Cecil

"The family is one of nature's masterpieces. It would be hard to conceive a system of instincts more nicely adjusted, where the constituents should represent or support one another better. The husband has an interest in protecting the wife, she in serving the husband. . . . Parents lend children their experience and a vicarious memory; children endow their parents with a vicarious immortality."

George Santayana: *The Life of Reason*

Kingdoms and empires have risen and fallen, but the family—the primary unit of human society—endures. It is the most durable and resilient institution that the human social instinct has ever invented. Historians tell us that the family has existed from time immemorial. It has prevailed in one form or another in human communities since prehistoric days. Because the records of those days are so hazy, archaeologists suggest that, just like herds among animals, human society began with great households.

It was the family, with its ties of affection and reciprocity, that refined and converted people into civilized human beings.

25

The Family in Ancient Times

Besides the dug-up remains and vestiges of vanished prehistoric days, evidence about family structures comes from the great poetic tradition embodied in the Homeric epics. From the Homeric poems, the *Iliad* and the *Odyssey*, we learn that the early Greeks centered their lives around their chiefs and heroes, who were the heads of families bound together by ties of love, discipline, and obedience. The whole plot of the *Iliad* is built around the stolen wife, Helen, and the violation of family honor. The goal of the entire *Odyssey* is the reuniting of Odysseus's family. It is the story of the wandering of Odysseus, finally reunited with his son Telemachus, and their vengeance on the suitors of Penelope, the wife of Odysseus and the mother of Telemachus. The gods in the two poems are always present and take part in the action. The Homeric gods marry goddesses who bear them children. They have family lives and family quarrels. Aristotle remarks in the *Politics* that people "assimilate the lives no less than the bodily forms of the gods to their own."

In the Classical Age of Greek history, the family was no less the center of social relationship. Oaths or other public acts implicated the family as well as the individual (other members of his family could be punished for a person's misdeeds), and the expulsion of an entire family from the *polis* was considered a fit punishment for treason or other such crimes. Family motives were also the inspiration for many patriotic endeavors and acts of service to the state. (Walter K. Lacey, *The Family in Classical Greece*, Cornell University Press, 1968, p. 33.)

In ancient Rome, too, the family was the primary social unit that gave strength to the state. In fact, the Romans saw themselves as one large family. The individual family mirrored the political concept of absolute domination by one person. The rights of the emperors set the pattern for the rights of the head of the family. The father of the family, the paterfamilias, wielded complete authority, including the power of life and death, over his children—a power similar to that of the monarch over the citizens of his empire. The family ruled by the paterfamilias even included slaves and servants. This paternal authority, known as the *patria potestas*, has been called the "fundamental institution of the Romans, which shaped and directed their world-view or *Weltanschauung*." (Beryl Rawson, ed., *The Family in Ancient Rome: New Perspectives*, Cornell University Press, 1987, p. 140.) It is not surprising that in the Latin tongue the words for father (*pater*) and country (*patria*) are so closely related.

The Judaeo-Christian Heritage

Since the American family structure is deeply rooted in the Judaeo-Christian cultural and religious tradition, the attitudes toward marriage and family expressed in the Old and New Testaments deserve special attention. This tradition emphasizes the family as the core of all social structure. In the Old Testament, after the Commandments about our obligations to God, the very next injunctions pertain to the honor due to parents and to the sanctity of marriage, which forbids adultery. The Hebrews' overarching emphasis on the family embraced concepts of family obligations, commitment, authority, sacrifice, integrity, and all the other shared values that lead to a healthy, secure, and productive life.

The criterion of righteousness for a man is that he preserves his family within "the way of the Lord," and family happiness is one of the rewards for those who fear the Lord. (Psalm 128:3, 6.)

The Old Testament includes illuminating records of patriarchal families from Abraham forward; for example, Jacob's twelve sons are the offspring of four different mothers. The proliferation of geneaologies within the Bible demonstrates the emphasis placed on bloodline, or lineal kinship. The importance accorded to the idea of family that went far beyond a single generation may be seen in the warning that the Lord is a jealous God, "visiting the iniquities of the fathers upon the children unto the third and fourth generations." (Exodus 20:5.)

In the New Testament, emphasis shifts somewhat toward the relationship between spouses and the nuclear family. Jesus' strictness about forbidding divorce stood in contrast to the compromises within existing Mosaic law. (Matthew 5:31-32.) According to the apostle Paul, pastoral responsibility required that the leader, or the "bishop," must be faithful to his one wife and that he must be a man of the highest principles, "who manages his household well and wins obedience from his children." (I Timothy 3:2-4.) A man is religious when "he and his whole family joined in the worship of God." (Acts 10:2.)

Although Christian tradition emphasizes the immediate bonds of the nuclear family, it also emphasizes the familial nature of all social relationship. For

Christians, the Son of God was born into a family, and his Sonship to God implies a family relationship among all believers—a relationship that even goes beyond an analogy with the ordinary family. "For whosoever shall do the will of God, the same is my brother and my sister and my mother." (Mark 3:35.)

The family is not merely the model of the ideal of all human relationships; it also becomes a metaphor for cosmic spiritual truths. The concept of the Trinity draws its terms from family relationship. St. Paul compares the relationship between husband and wife to the relationship between Christ and the church, which is His body. For conjugal unity a man shall leave his parents and be joined to his wife, "and the two shall become a single body." In this unity, Paul writes, "a great truth is hidden." (Ephesians 5:31–32.) The idea of the family achieved a new dignity as it was filtered through the Judaeo-Christian tradition.

The Family and the "State of Nature"

The moral climate of the Dark Ages, which followed the collapse of the Roman Empire, did not favor the emergence of a systematic theory about the nuclear family, rooted in human love and the affirmation of children. However, at the dawn of modern times—marked by the advent of the Renaissance, the discovery of America, and the Reformation—the family question occupied the thoughts of many philosophers and historians. Jean Bodin (1530–1596) and Francisco Suarez (1548–1617) were two, among others, who sought to examine the relationship of the state and the family.

Bodin, the French social and political philosopher who was the first to develop the doctrine of national sovereignty, traced the origin of the state to the family. The family, according to Bodin, is the natural social unit from which the state arises; the state is nothing else but a group of families subjected to one and the same rule. The sovereignty of the state, however, is distinct from the power of the father of a family.

What distinguishes the family from the state, writes Bodin, is the fact that the state has "the final and public authority," while in the family, children and serfs are joined by the "limited and private rule" of the father. Bodin defines the *summum imperium,* or sovereignty, as a supreme, absolute power over citizens and subjects, unrestrained by human law and vested in the person of the monarch. The father of a family has only "private authority" or "domestic rule" that holds together his wife, children, and serfs. (Bodin, *Method for the Easy Comprehension of History,* trans. by Beatrice Reynolds, W.W. Norton Company, 1969, pp. 157–158.)

Francisco Suarez, a Spanish Jesuit theologian, achieved a prominent position in the history of political thought through his theories of social contract and natural law. He made a distinction between natural law, which is fundamentally divine, and the "municipal," or "civil," law that each nation establishes for itself. Natural law is revealed to us by the light of reason and remains in essential agreement with the constitution of human nature.

In his book *De legibus,* Suarez maintains that the family is the most fundamental natural society, but it is not self-sufficient. To preserve public order and peace between individual families, nature demands the establishment of the state and of political sovereignty. The state is a political community formed by a coalition of families. The establishment of laws is the main function of the government and the essential nature of political sovereignty. The family remains the perfect community for purposes of domestic government, while the state is a perfect political community. (King James I of England had Suarez's book *De defensione fidei* burned because of the Jesuit's teaching that earthly power is held by the whole people and that kingly power is derived from them.)

Natural law is based on the eternal standard of righteousness that God inscribed on the heart of every person and that enables each individual to know truth from falsehood and good from evil. Among those who unfolded the concept of natural law, the most distinguished was the English political philosopher John Locke (1632–1704), who greatly influenced Thomas Jefferson with his ideas about social contract and the state of nature. All men, Locke maintains, are "naturally" in the state of nature and remain so until by their own consent they make themselves members of some political society. In this state, the family—the primary form of human society—fulfills the needs of the essential and uniform nature of human beings. Locke's social contract theory argues that sovereignty resides in the people, who have the moral right to overthrow a government that does not reflect the popular will.

Attacks by Collectivism and Individualism

Over the last 200 years, we have witnessed two great assaults against the primacy of the family unit as the basic building block of society—the trends toward collectivism and toward individualism. Both of these trends have tended to loosen the glue that keeps families together, and both have their roots in the work of the political philosophers of the modern era. As one political scientist has expressed it:

> "The attack on the family in modern political thought has been sweeping and unremitting. Although the critiques vary in their intensity, dissatisfaction with the family is nearly universal in modern political thought—so much so that the family as an institutional form has come to be regarded as one of the central problems of political philosophy." (Philip Abbott, *The Family on Trial: Special Relationships in Modern Political Thought*, Pennsylvania State University Press, 1981, p. 4.)

A. *Collectivism*

The collectivist trend has been the more dramatic historically. In its various forms over the last two centuries, the totalitarian state has aggressively tried to destroy the tradition of family life by assuming that the child is a mere creature of the state. For a short time during the French Revolution, the family was virtually abolished as far as law was concerned. The Jacobins, with their theory that a legitimate society is founded on the *contrat-social*, or social pact, believed in the total alienation of each individual, with all his rights, from familial loyalties. They believed that the state, as omnipotent sovereign and universal proprietor, should take "all things and persons" into its hands, since it "exercises at discretion its boundless rights over persons and things." (H.A. Taine, *The French Revolution*, Vol. III, Peter Smith, 1954, p. 54.)

According to Jean-Jacques Rousseau, the political theorist with the most influence over the Jacobins, "As nature gives each man absolute power over all his members, the social compact gives the body politic absolute power over all its members also." (*The Social Contract*, trans. by G.D.H. Cole, E.P. Dutton & Co., 1950, p. 28.) Jean-Baptiste Carrier, in presenting the Jacobin program at the time of the French Revolution, proclaimed, "We will make France a cemetery rather than not regenerate it our own way." (Taine, p. 61.)

In the nineteenth century, Marxist theory again launched an assault on the ideal of the family. *The Communist Manifesto* of 1848 promised that "the bourgeois family will disappear" and that "domestic education" would be replaced by a "social" one in order to withdraw education "from the influence of the ruling class." (*The Communist Manifesto of Karl Marx and Friedrich Engels*, Russell & Russell, 1963, p. 48.) Friedrich Engels in his 1884 treatise *The Origin of the Family, Private Property and the State* writes:

> "With the transfer of the means of production into common ownership, the single family ceases to be the economic unit of society. Private housekeeping is transformed into a social industry. The care and edu-

cation of the children becomes a public affair; society looks after all children alike, whether they are legitimate or not." (International Publishers, 1972, p. 139.)

This worldview sees reproduction as a purely sexual function requiring no emotional, durable union of the two parents, nor does it provide a place for parental love. It envisions that children will be reared by the state (*in loco parentis*) to serve its purposes.

In our generation we have witnessed that the attempts to turn this theory into practice have fortunately been short-lived. In the Soviet Union, the Bolshevik Revolution aspired to abolish the family and to substitute for it a universal, state-controlled orphanage. In Joseph Stalin's Soviet Russia, children proved their patriotic loyalty by denouncing their parents to the secret police. The horrors of Stalin's own personal family life were revealed in the memoirs of his daughter, Svetlana Alliluyeva. As the prominent American philosopher George Santayana points out, "it is conceivable that a communist, abolishing the family in order to make opportunities equal and remove the more cruel injustices of fortune, might be drying up that milk of human kindness which had fed his own enthusiasm." (*Reason in Society*, Dover Publishing Company, 1980, p. 47.)

For decades the family lives of Soviet leaders remained under a cloud of mystery. Their spouses remained virtually invisible and rarely appeared in public. It became known to the public that Yuri Andropov had a wife only when she showed up at his 1984 funeral. (With Gorbachev's *glasnost* came also the one-woman revolution—his wife, Raisa, is not only the most visible leader's wife since the fall of the Romanoffs but also her husband's closest adviser.)

Whether we attribute the failure to the vestiges of Christian ways of life deeply rooted in the Russian people or to the natural human instinct binding together individuals forming a family, the Communist Party's aspiration to abolish the family in the Soviet Union was rejected and never fulfilled. In China, as well, Mao Tse-tung's doctrines did not succeed in destroying the traditional fabric of family life. By creating a universal orphanage, Mao hoped to transform Chinese political, social, and economic tradition. He failed because he underestimated the strength of the 3,000-year-old Chinese civilization, with its emphasis on the family. This tradition embraces not only family unity but also the concepts of humility, responsibility, mutual respect, and kindness and encourages the sharing of burdens and benefits.

The totalitarian assault on family life has not been limited to communist countries. In Hitler's Germany, too, children proved their loyalty to the party by rejecting the authority inherent in the parent-child relationship, by accepting the exclusive authority of the fuehrer, and by pulling back from or breaking with the family of which they were a part.

B. Individualism

The other trend in the history of recent decades has been toward an individualism that often rebels against the sacrosanct concepts of family life. Under the pressure of circumstances—especially because of the con-

stant growth of individual liberty in the Western world—
family life has found itself subjected to changes in cultural mores and in legal structures that weaken the traditional authority of parents. One analysis of these changes
contends that

> "the key to understanding the recent upheavals in
> family life lies in a profound shift in cultural values.
> Three decades ago most Americans shared certain
> strong attitudes about the family. Public opinion
> polls showed that they endorsed marriage as a pre-
> requisite of well-being, social adjustment, and ma-
> turity and agreed on the proper roles of husband and
> wife. . . . Values and norms have shifted. The watch-
> words of contemporary society are 'growth,' 'self-
> realization,' and 'fulfillment.'" (Steven Mintz and
> Susan Kellogg, *Domestic Revolutions: A Social
> History of American Family Life*, The Free Press,
> 1988, p. 205.)

These changes, however, are not necessarily a mere
tinkering with the holy institutions that protect the family. Some of these changes encourage a more sensitive
consideration of the personal interests of husband and
wife and their needs for individuality, as well as more
freedom for their children in choosing their own careers
and associations—all without abolishing a basic reliance
on family ties.

Only when the selfish desires of the individual cannot
be reconciled with the essential requirements of the family group is the strength of the family threatened. Only
when extreme individualism overrides everything that
is cherished in family life is the family structure crip-

pled. Only when the concept of the family is corrupted by embracing such alternatives as group marriages, homosexual marriages, children deliberately conceived out of wedlock, and other forms of cultural nihilism can we say that the characteristic values of family life are disintegrating and collapsing. Such signs as undisciplined self-gratification, addiction to alcohol and other drugs, promiscuity, facile divorce, and the rising numbers of runaway children demonstrate the large numbers of individuals alienated from family relationships in our society.

The Early American Family

Collectivism and undisciplined individualism destroy the kind of freedom and support that the tutelage of a family at its best can give. In fact, a totalitarian system must destroy this tutelage because the mutual respect, loyalty, and love of family members—based on accepted tenets of morality and traditional standards of conduct—are the manifestation of a free society rooted in family and resting on a profound set of historic values. A free society resting on historic values cannot be tolerated by dictators.

It was Alexis de Tocqueville who observed that American democracy rests on such values. His book *Democracy in America* keeps amazing its readers with the profundity of its author's observations concerning the great American experiment that marked a new epoch in the world's history. Tocqueville's observations are not limited to the new economic, social, and political realities of the young nation. He illuminates also the ways in which the American ideal influenced the cornerstone of American democracy—the American family.

The American family, as Tocqueville describes it, dif-
fered from the European family of the same period. In
the early nineteenth century, the European family was
strongly paternalistic, bound by laws controlling the de-
scent of property (directing most of the property to the
oldest son) and by customs demanding the obedience of
adult children to the will of their parents. The father was
not only the head of the family but "also its magistrate."
(*Democracy in America*, trans. by George Lawrence,
Harper & Row, 1966, p. 561.)

As described by Tocqueville, the American family
seemed also to differ from the pattern of the English
family that we have come to think of as Victorian, with
its evangelical patriarchal structure that stressed piety
within the family and was based on obedience, respect,
and the recognition of the powerful role of family prayer
in training children and servants. The American family,
in contrast, expected children to be independent almost
from adolescence. As Tocqueville puts it, "In America
there is in truth no adolescence. At the close of boyhood
a young person is a man and begins to trace out his own
path." (*Id.*, p. 560.) Furthermore, the laws of democracy
conduced to break up paternalistic authority. Tocqueville claims that "in democracies, where the long arm of
government reaches each particular man among the
crowd separately to bend him to obedience to the common laws, there is no need for . . . an intermediary. In the
eyes of the law the father is only a citizen older and richer
than his sons." (*Id.*, p. 561.)

Although the legal ties that bound families together
were more rigid in Europe than in America, families in
America developed much stronger ties of affection and

sentiment than their European counterparts. "Not inter-est, then, but common memories and the unhampered sympathy of thoughts and tastes draw brothers, in a democracy, to one another. Their inheritance is divided, but their hearts are free to unite." (*Id.*, p. 564.)

In the early nineteenth century, the status of women in the United States was unique. In the great novels of Henry James, whose favorite subject matter was the con-trast between Europeans and Americans of the leisure class, the figure of the independent American young woman—of whom Daisy Miller is only the most famous—caused consternation and admiration in equal measure among her European acquaintances. Earlier, Tocque-ville had explained the idea of a young American woman who was both independent and virtuous—an idea that seemed strange to members of older and more rigid so-cieties—as follows: "Unable to prevent her chastity from being often in danger, they want her to know how to defend herself, and they count on the strength of her free determination more than on safeguards which have been shaken or overthrown." (*Id.*, p. 566.) Consequently, Amer-ican girls were better educated and much more widely experienced than their European counterparts.

This changing role of women in American society in the early years of our nation had important ramifi-cations both in family life and in the life of the nation. Whereas in Europe during this period most marriages were still the product of parental arrangement, in the United States the young woman reared to be indepen-dent expected to have her say in the choice of her hus-band. Surprisingly enough, in order to create a strong sense of family and to serve as an example of high purity of morals, the married American woman of this period was expected to be centered on domestic activity much more than was her European counterpart.

How did a young woman sacrifice her independence to accept these familial duties? Tocqueville explains that the very liberty the American woman had in choosing her fate prepared her to meet the challenges of married life willingly. "One may say," he writes, "that it is the very enjoyment of freedom that has given her the courage to sacrifice it without struggle or complaint when the time has come for that. . . . She knows beforehand what will be expected of her, and she herself has freely accepted the yoke." (*Id.*, p. 568.) In recognition of her sacrifices the Congress that convened on February 4, 1914, declared a national Mother's Day.

This pattern of liberty for the individual coupled with a sense of duty both familial and social provided the United States in the early nineteenth century with a moral atmosphere in which these duties were performed. The virtues of duty and earnestness that originated in the nuclear American family had covert political implications since they spread from the home into society, producing a stability centered around the ideals of public virtue combined with private morality. Tocqueville contrasts this American atmosphere with the situation in his own country. "During the last fifty years of transformation France has rarely known freedom, disorder always. In the universal confusion of thought undermining all established concepts, incoherently jumbling right and wrong, truth and falsehood, law and fact, public virtue has become unreliable and private morality shaken." (*Id.*, p. 574.)

The Contemporary American Family

The normal, or ideal, nuclear American family is usually thought of as consisting of a father, a mother, and their children, all living together and united by love, common values, and legal protection for the spouse and children. In the United States of the 1990s, however, not all households actually conform to this pattern. The rising incidence of divorce and single parenthood, the postponement of marriage and childbearing, and the shrinking size of the nuclear family have all contributed to shaking the foundation of the "typical" family. Does this network of profound social changes mean that the familial ideals that characterized many generations of philosophical thought and the remarkable developments and achievements of American family life in the early years of our country no longer have any relevance to family life in our society?

On the contrary, the ideals of family life developed through the growth of Western civilization and embodied in the traditions of American families since before the days of Tocqueville still have great relevance to us today. The American family retains the resilience to resist attacks both from the side of totalitarian collectivism and from the side of extreme individualism. The U.S. Supreme Court has repeatedly rejected the totalitarian idea that the child is the creature of the state. On one occasion, it referred to the ideal state Plato conceived in his *Republic* in which the rulers of the state (the "Guardians") would hold wives and children in common and in which parents and children would not know each other. The Court categorically rejected such a system—as well as policies like the one of Sparta that assembled males at the age of seven into barracks and entrusted their education to official guardians—by stating that "although such measures have been deliberately approved by men of great genius, their ideas touching the relation between individual and state were wholly different from those on which our institutions rest." (*Meyer v. State of Nebraska*, 43 S. Ct. 625, 628 [1923].)

Family Laws

The continuing place of the family in our society is revealed by the laws that regulate marriage and family life, since the state remains greatly concerned with preserving traditional family relationships. Entry into marriage is a contract between the parties, but the state has an important interest in the marriage relationship. Various laws, both common and statutory, regulate consanguinity, property, inheritance, and other rights, duties, and obligations fixed by the family contract, which can be dissolved only for what the state deems proper grounds.

In the United States numerous laws favor the formal family. In almost all states, inheritance laws convey a decedent's estate to the next of kin in the absence of testamentary instructions from the deceased person. In some states the so-called community property principle provides marital interests in real property regardless of whether both spouses' names are on the title. Personal injury laws (known as "wrongful death laws") confer upon the family members of a person killed by someone's intentional or negligent act the right to sue the person who caused the death. Such preferential treatment, reflecting the social policy of reinforcing formal family relationships, is not given to other relationships.

The increasing trend toward recognizing the rights of illegitimate children does not reflect a change in this policy. This trend was prompted by the realization that the punishment of innocent children is unfair and is not effective in pursuing society's interests in discouraging illegitimate births. In spite of the growing openness of couples cohabiting outside marriage, the formal, legal family remains the bedrock concept of our legal and social system.

The legal family—based on accepted tenets of morality and traditional standards of conduct—is the source of the legal fiction that husband and wife are one person. In order not to disturb family harmony, the common-law rule, accepted at an early date as applicable in this country, was that husband and wife are incompetent as witnesses for or against each other. In *Funk v. United States* (54 S. Ct. 212 [1933]) the Supreme Court rejected the principle of the common law that excluded testimony by spouses for each other but continued to bar testimony of one spouse against the other in the belief "that such a policy was necessary to foster family peace, not only for the benefit of a husband, wife and children, but for the benefit of the public as well." (*Hawkins v. United States*, 79 S. Ct. 136, 138 [1958].) Most states retain the rule, though it has been subject to modifications and many states provide exceptions in some classes of case. The limited nature of these exceptions can be explained by

the widespread belief that the law should not force testimony that "might alienate husband or wife, or further
inflame existing domestic differences." (*Id.*, p. 139.)

Keynote Principles of the Family's Strength

In the United States as well as in other countries belonging to the Free World, free love and easy divorce
(as in the case of no-fault divorce laws in many states)
tend to threaten the family institution without proposing
any substitute for the family, which Will Durant calls
the "nucleus of civilization." Some changes in the forms
and direction of the family are beyond the individual's
control. Family life has become a casualty of the mobility, urbanization, and industrialization that have weakened the old economic rationales of mutual dependence
and support as well as the quality of the family relationship. Mobility, which can widely scatter members of a
family, disintegrates the natural family, since it can no
longer function as the traditional family once did. Urbanization and industrialization have broken down the
organized work-unit characteristic of, if not indispensable to, farming or running artisan and small-business
shops.

The family's circle tends to include only the nuclear
family, with no place for old people or other members
of the extended family. Older people, once considered
an asset, are often perceived as a burden and as a limitation on the family's freedom as its members move to
new places where better employment opportunities are
offered.

A. Loyalty

What remains within our control, however, is the possibility of a revival of the strength and vitality of the underlying principles of the traditional family that can counteract the forces that debilitate this institution. One of these principles is family loyalty. This principle is universal, existing in all cultures. It exalts high purposes, deep feelings of warm affection, self-discipline, and often self-denial. It involves common thoughts and purposes and binds together individuals who are faced with conflicting loyalties.

History provides many examples both of family loyalty and of conflicting loyalties. The most famous biblical passage dealing with a conflict between loyalty to the family and other loyalties is the story of King David and his son Absalom. Absalom was the favorite not only of his father but of many others in the kingdom—his splendid personal appearance and charm assured his great popularity. Banished from the court because he contrived the death of his half-brother Amnon (who had criminally dishonored Absalom's sister Tamar), Absalom upon his return from exile at Geshur gathered followers who proclaimed him king in rivalry to his own father. David fled in panic from Jerusalem with a few faithful friends. Absalom's failure to pursue his father immediately—a delay secured by David's counselor Husahi, who pretended to support Absalom—saved David's life as well as his throne.

In the crucial battle that eventually ensued, Absalom was defeated and in his flight was caught by his long hair in the thick boughs of an oak and slain by the hand of

David's military chief, Joab. David's lament over his son—"O my son Absalom, my son, my son Absalom! would God I had died for thee, O Absalom, my son, my son!"—became one of the most moving passages of scripture and was even given musical settings by many composers throughout the years. Joab rebuked David for turning victory into mourning, a rebuke that had political significance. He accused David of "hating his friends and loving his enemies," of showing loyalty to his unfaithful son rather than to his friends and to the countrymen who had remained loyal to him and saved his life, the lives of his family members, and his throne.

The foremost psychologist in the field of childhood and adolescent development, Erik H. Erikson, stresses the importance of the development of a sense of loyalty in the adolescent years. He maintains that a sense of fervent fidelity to a cause or idea is one of the most characteristic virtues of a youth, and emphasizes that it is the task of the family and of society to nurture that virtue and direct it to the service of worthy ends. Only when that sense of loyalty or fidelity is properly fostered is an adolescent ready for adult commitments.

> "'Loyal' and 'legal' have the same root, linguistically and psychologically; for legal commitment is an unsafe burden unless shouldered with a sense of sovereign choice and experienced as loyalty. To develop that sense is a joint task of the consistency of individual life history and the ethical potency of the historical process." ("Youth: Fidelity and Diversity" in *The Challenge of Youth*, ed. by Erik H. Erikson, Anchor Books, 1965, p. 4.)

To develop such a sense of loyalty to the common good, especially to the family itself, is one of the primary tasks of family life.

Family loyalty calls for solidarity. The bloodline, or genetic inheritance, turns the family into a multigenerational institution that encompasses not only the immediate generations of children and parents but also ancestors and generations of descendants to come. When, for instance, our national debt is discussed, concern is expressed about its burdening impact on future generations. The common obligation of solidarity extends to the sick, poor, and helpless members of the family. Older people cannot be treated as incidentals, like old pieces of furniture to be stored in an old-age home.

Disregard of family solidarity results in self-centeredness and a life of self-gratification deprived of noble purposes. The family and its entity may be a part of our social instinct, but it cannot be taken for granted. Loyalty, which is the fruit of caring and sharing, does not thrive spontaneously. Rather, it must be cultivated continuously or it will be debilitated by the forces causing intense strains and stress on family relationships.

B. *Parental Love and Authority*

The second principle indispensable to the proper functioning of the family is parental love and acceptance of parental authority. Children are like mirrors to their parents, who hope that heirs will fulfill their foiled ambitions. As Santayana expresses it, "Man's soul may more truly survive in his son's youth than in his own decrepitude," and in order to give our children a proper place in this world, we are ready to "commit the blotted manuscript of our lives more willingly to the flames, when we find the immortal text already half engrossed in a fairer copy." (*Reason in Society*, pp. 6, 42.) The child finds security in parental love as well as in parental authority.

In modern America, an emphasis on the proper use of parental authority can seem old-fashioned and out of place. It is true that the most ancient and traditional sources of moral inspiration stress the importance of parental authority. The Bible, as noted earlier, makes the obedience children owe to parents one of the most basic commandments: "Honor thy father and thy mother." (Exodus 20:12.) For those who fail to live up to this precept, Mosaic law imposes a curse: "For every one that curseth his father or his mother shall be surely put to death: he has cursed his father or his mother; his blood shall be upon him." (Leviticus 20:9.) In the New Testament, the language is milder, but the sentiments are no less sure: "Children, obey your parents in the Lord: for this is right. Honor thy father and mother, which is the first commandment with promise." (Ephesians 6:1–2.)

But the concept that parental authority is a necessary force in any society is not solely religious. Many modern social thinkers are beginning to admit that such authority is essential. Brigitte and Peter L. Berger contrast two possible solutions to the problems of young people in America today. One, which they reject, is the increasing intrusiveness of outside "helpers" (whether educational or psychological experts). They believe that such impersonal authorities are bound to be less effective than the natural authorities lying much closer to hand:

"The other possible solution is to seek ways to re-assert the emotional and moral primacy of the family. Politically, this means to reassert the authority of parents, of whatever class, against both school and youth culture. Movements such as Moral Majority are only the extreme expression of this reassertion. There is a much broader view that parents must regain control over their growing children. It is strong in all classes . . . and has been particularly strong among racial and ethnic minorities (where parents have felt impotent in the face of arrogant educational authorities and a particularly troublesome youth culture)." (*The War Over the Family: Capturing the Middle Ground,* Anchor Press/Doubleday, 1983, pp. 161–162.)

Such sentiments are not limited to American thinkers. A pair of German sociologists recently published a study that came to a remarkably similar conclusion:

"But even when a further decrease in family functions brings further emancipation, as is to be expected, there is one relationship to which this can never fully apply: the relationship between parents and children. As a social form that gives protection, the family must always have a head; as a socializing agent, it must always be able to exercise authority." (Michael Mitterauer and Reinhard Sieder, *The European Family: Patriarchy to Partnership from the Middle Ages to the Present,* trans. by Karla Ooster-veen and Manfred Hoerzinger, The University of Chicago Press, 1982, p. 89.)

In the final analysis, it is the parents, not any external authority, who bear the responsibility for inculcating a sense of discipline and a recognition of the rights of other individuals and the society at large within the children of a family. In his book *Haven in a Heartless World*, sociologist Christopher Lasch reviews the ways in which all too many American families have abandoned this primary responsibility to outside agencies—often with the best of intentions, under the assumption that "expert" educators, psychologists, and the like know better than the families do how to raise their children. "The confusion of parents dependent on professional theories of child rearing, their reluctance to exercise authority or to assume responsibility for the child's development, and the delegation of discipline to various outside agencies have already diluted the quality of child care...." (*Haven in a Heartless World: The Family Besieged*, Basic Books, 1977, p. 123.)

Such a misguided abdication of parental responsibility can have results as disastrous as those of the totalitarian stripping of parental authority; in both cases, the end result is that an outside agency, rather than the home, has the ultimate responsibility for the lives of the children. The family suffers when moral values fall victim to negligence and indifference on the part of parents who transfer the responsibility of raising children to schools or other agencies of society.

The idea of the natural authority of parents and of the respect due them does not imply the sort of power over life and death that fathers had in ancient Rome, nor does it imply the complete authority of the patriarchal family. Discipline should not be confused with regimentation. Discipline is in accord with acceptance of the worth and dignity of every member in the family unit; regimentation gives rise to rebellion. Discipline gives every member of the family the right to shape his or her destiny, while regimentation is a cause of irritation and friction.

Respect for parents grows with maturity. We are reminded of Mark Twain's observation that at eighteen he thought his father was stupid but when he reached age twenty-one he was amazed by how smart his father had become in three years. Parental authority does not call for rigid formality in the parent-child relationship. In contrast, it may become the main avenue for the pursuit of domestic happiness.

Tocqueville points out the deep difference between a loveless patriarchy and the new American family resting on equality: "But among democratic nations every word a son addresses to his father has a tang of freedom, familiarity, and tenderness all at once, which gives an immediate impression of the new relationship prevailing in the family." (*Democracy in America*, p. 563.)

The union of love and authority is an essential corollary to the preservation of the traditional family. Through a judicious use of authority children learn to mold themselves into the image of their parents. Parents need children, and children need parents. Because of this mutual need that is the lifeblood of a harmonious family, parents cannot be replaced by state nurseries or school counselors.

The family deserves its autonomy (within the rule of the state sustaining the values of family ties) only if parents provide the moral climate that will enable their children to determine the meaning and purpose of their lives. This leads us to the third among other principles underlying the strength and vitality of the traditional family—the principle of commitment.

C. *Comprehensive Commitment*

This principle of comprehensive commitment embraces the covenant "for richer, for poorer, in sickness and in health, till death do us part." Frequently these days, a child lives in a family where there is only one parent or where one of the parents is a stepparent, not because of death but because of divorce. According to the Central Bureau of Statistics in Stockholm, 50 percent of all couples living together in Sweden have preferred not to get married. In twenty-five years, children born of unwed mothers have increased from 10 percent of the total born to 50 percent. Marriage has become weakened as a social institution. (*Sweden Now*, 3/1988, Vol. 22, p. 14.) According to social analysts, a large percentage of those marrying in the United States in recent decades do not expect to remain married to that partner. When a decision to get married is made with an eye on possible divorce, the whole structure of family life is imperiled.

The principle of commitment rejects the idea of "non-binding commitments" that advocate "open marriage" and other theories that exalt companionship as the sole essence of married life and leave the rearing of children to the state. Such a comprehensive commitment extends beyond the preservation of togetherness "under one roof" of the blood-tied nucleus of man, woman, and offspring. Under this commitment, the traditional family in order to survive must also transmit to each new generation values of decency, propriety, honesty, and fidelity and the rules and principles that relate to right and wrong conduct. Family life becomes crippled when it is deprived of the "moral sense" that gives family members the power to distinguish between right and wrong.

The Sanctity of the Home

Rapid changes are taking place in our society. They have brought attacks against established ideas and institutions, including the traditional family. These assaults, focused mainly on hedonism and escape from family responsibilities, have been the subject of controversy but should not cause alarm. The emotional intensity that has always characterized family relations will not be drained by these assaults since the family institution rests on a solid base of religious and historic values deeply rooted in human life.

In reality the importance of family life and the sanctity of the home have always remained dominant values in our society. During the 1988 national political conventions, the presidential and vice-presidential candidates stressed the importance of familial affection by displaying mothers, fathers, wives, children, and grandchildren. The candidates kept assuring prospective voters that their families were their strength, pride, joy, love, and "total life" (Dan Quayle in his convention speech). Jesse Jackson was introduced by all five of his children. According to *Time* magazine, "The unit of measure, and manipulation, in politics is no longer the citizen. It is the family." (Charles Krauthammer, "Spare Us the Family Album," *Time*, September 19, 1988, p. 104).

Whether this show of devotion to family was a part of the political game or truly reflected a trend toward returning to domesticity and family life, the fact remains that there is no reason to despair about the problems facing our families: the revolt of the yuppies and the baby boomers, the divorce crisis, the tragedy of shattered inner-city families, the rhetoric of radical feminism, and the large numbers of children living with single parents. Nothing has ever been built on pessimism. Instead of despair, we should seek avenues to which we have to channel our efforts to revitalize the strength of the family as an institution.

Numerous remedies are available to counteract in responsible ways the forces that debilitate the ties and the moral climate of family life. Among those remedies central to the proper functions of the family are the three we have been discussing—loyalty, parental love and authority, and commitment. Only if these three keynote principles are abandoned will the "sacredness" of marriage and the home cease to be our main hope for joy and the principal place in which we carry out the pursuit of happiness our heritage promises us.

VIRTUE, FAMILIES, AND CITIZENSHIP

by

Mary Ann Glendon

Mary Ann Glendon

Mary Ann Glendon, a Professor of Law at Harvard University since 1986, writes and teaches in the fields of comparative law, property, and legal theory. In 1988, she won the Scribes Book Award given by the American Society of Writers on Legal Subjects for her comparative study, Abortion and Divorce in Western Law. *Professor Glendon taught at Boston College Law School from 1968 to 1986, and has been a visiting professor from time to time at the University of Chicago Law School.*

She received her Bachelor of Arts, Juris Doctor, and Master of Comparative Law degrees from the University of Chicago, where she was awarded the American Jurisprudence Prize for first place in civil law and a two-year fellowship to study French law at the University of Chicago and the Universite Libre de Bruxelles. In 1963 Professor Glendon was a legal intern with the European Economic Community in Brussels, and from 1963 to 1968 she practiced law with the Chicago firm of Mayer, Brown & Platt.

Professor Glendon has written over forty articles and book chapters and has lectured widely in this country and in Europe. She has published seven books, including The Transformation of Family Law *(1989),* Abortion and Divorce in Western Law *(1987),* The New Family and the New Property *(1981), and a casebook on comparative legal traditions. She has received honorary LL.D. degrees from the College of the Holy Cross and Seton Hall University Law School and an honorary Doctor of Humane Letters degree from Brigham Young University.*

Her service activities include membership on the Cardinal's Advisory Committee on Social Justice in the Archdiocese of Boston, as well as on the boards of several charitable and legal organizations.

VIRTUE, FAMILIES, AND CITIZENSHIP

by

Mary Ann Glendon

The general title for this lecture series, "The Meaning of the Family in a Free Society," has an air of lofty serenity about it. Like the old adage "a sound mind in a healthy body," it calls up an image of right ordering in a functioning system. The same might be said for my own title, "Virtue, Families, and Citizenship," which may appear to you not only serene but soporific. Underneath these high-sounding words representing so many of our individual and collective ideals, however, a tremendous ferment is taking place. This ferment is so intense that many are calling it a "culture struggle"—a contest being waged within the United States over the fundamental understandings of what kind of society we are and the role of common moral intuitions in contributing to those understandings. The culture struggle is being prosecuted on many fronts, but nowhere more intensely than in what sociologists Brigitte and Peter Berger have called "the war over the family."

What is the war over the family? According to the Bergers, it is "a vociferous debate over the history, the present condition, the prospects and, most important, the human and societal value of the family"—in other words, over "the meaning of the family." By this light, then, the title of this year's Cecil lecture series is not so peaceful after all. My intent, however, is not to join in

the fray but to suggest a reformulation of the terms of
the debate. Let me begin, therefore, with some thumb-
nail sketches of the four high-profile positions in the conflict over "the meaning of the family in a free society."
For purposes of these sketches, I will make a distinction
between economic and cultural progressives and between economic and cultural conservatives. Like all cap-
sule summaries, my characterizations will be somewhat
oversimplified, but it is worthwhile to state the positions
initially in their pure forms.

(1) On the cultural right we find the defenders of what
people in those circles are apt to call the "traditional"
family, imagined as a household founded on a marriage
between a husband-breadwinner and a wife-homemaker.

(2) On the cultural left, the same household is apt to be
called the "patriarchal" family. Over here, we find people claiming that an oppressive male-dominated society
made the "traditional" family into a totem, while system-
atically subordinating women. The remedy, for some, is
to abolish the very concept of family in favor of treating
the *individual* as the basic social unit. Others would
expand "family" to include so many different types of
relationships that the word loses all meaning.

(3) On the economic right, claiming that family poverty and related social ills actually worsened over the period
of greatest governmental attention to them, conservatives like Charles Murray have advocated a laissez-faire
family policy as a spur to self-reliance.

(4) On the economic left, by contrast, the same problems are believed to require redoubled public efforts to
aid families, with government taking over many of the

tasks that family members no longer find easy to perform.

One may sum up these four approaches as the totem vs. the taboo on the culture front and the heartless vs. the ham-handed on the economic front. Though the positions, in policy terms, are usually opposed, they have in common the fact that those who hold them rarely make the connection (suggested by the title of this lecture series) between the state of American family life and the problem of maintaining a free society. That is, if asked to explain why families are important, persons on both ends of the political spectrum are apt to give similar answers: healthy families enable individuals to develop their full potential; families are the main source of the work force upon we which we depend for our social security system and our competitive position in the world economy; dysfunctional families breed delinquency and crime. All of these concerns are undeniably important. But it is fair to say that in the war over the family, the existence of a free society is usually just assumed as part of the background.

Thus we do not hear much about two questions that ought to be at the very forefront of current debates about the family and family policy: (1) Given our commitment, from the eighteenth century onward, to a historic experiment in ordered liberty, where are we to find citizens capable of sustaining, and actively participating in, the venture of democratic self-government? (2) Given our commitment since the 1930s to a form of welfare state, where are we to find citizens with enough sense of fellow feeling to reach out to others in need, yet enough sense of personal responsibility to assume substantial control over their own lives? These are the problems I would like to explore with you in this lecture.

In raising these questions, I am, of course, doing no more than starting where the classical political philosophers did—with nurture and education. If history teaches us anything, it is that a "free society" is not just a given; that there seem to be conditions that are more, or less, favorable to freedom; and that these conditions importantly involve character—the character of individual citizens and the character of those who serve the public in legislative, executive, judicial, or administrative capacities. Character, it hardly needs to be said, cannot be assumed either. It, too, has conditions— residing in nurture and education. Thus one can hardly escape from acknowledging the political importance of the family. Yet this is a subject on which participants in "the war over the family" are strangely silent.

Social historians of the future no doubt will be bemused by the fact that we late-twentieth-century Americans found it acceptable, even fashionable, to publicly discuss in detail the most intimate aspects of personal life, while maintaining an almost prudish reserve concerning the political significance of family life. If those social historians are French (as so many of them have been so far), they will probably not be able to resist pointing out that a French visitor to the United States laid it all out for us—up to a point—in the 1830s. One reason Alexis de Tocqueville still seems to be so important for our self-understanding is that, almost alone, he carried forward the insights of the great classical political philosophers into the modern era. He tried to figure out how these insights could be applied under historically novel circumstances, in democracies committed to equality and individual liberty. Tocqueville,

as is well-known, regarded families as crucial to the
preservation of a free society. But it is worthwhile re-
calling why he thought so. looking at the democratic
experiments being undertaken in America and Europe
in the nineteenth century, he accurately forecast that
the key question was whether they would yield equality
in freedom or equality in servitude. If democratic nations should fail in "imparting to all citizens those ideas
and sentiments which first prepare them for freedom
and then allow them to enjoy it," he warned, "there will
be no independence left for anybody, . . . neither for the
poor nor for the rich, but only an equal tyranny for all.
. . ." The prospects for a given country, he said, would
depend somewhat on its physical situation, and even
more on its laws. Most of all, though, Tocqueville said,
a free society would be sustained by its mores, by which
he meant "the whole moral and intellectual state of a
people."

So, from the point of view suggested by Tocqueville,
the problem of how to preserve a free and democratic republic becomes the question of what tends to nourish the
practices and attitudes that make freedom possible.
Here is where the family comes in, for to Tocqueville it
seemed plain that the required habits and beliefs were
being taught and transmitted from generation to generation within American families and chiefly by women,
who were the main teachers of children and the "keepers
of orderly peaceful homes." Here, one would have to say
with hindsight, is one of the rare instances where the
great observer seems to have nodded. Like so many other
high-minded nineteenth-century intellectuals, Tocqueville just took for granted that the family was one of the

few remaining institutions that would be able to moderate the effects of individual greed, selfishness, and ambition. Yet there is a puzzle here. No one had seen more deeply than he into how powerful currents of individualism and egalitarianism were transforming all traditional social arrangements. Why, one wonders, did he not pursue the logic of his own analysis and realize that not even family life could remain unaffected?

The answer seems to be that Tocqueville (like many of his contemporaries) made what seemed to him a self-evident distinction between bonds that were merely legal or social and those he called "natural." It seemed obvious to him that family ties were natural and, as such, much less subject to disruption by the winds of change than, say, the relations between master and servant. Thus, Tocqueville could write that, in general, "Democracy loosens social ties, but it tightens natural ones. At the same time that it separates citizens, it brings kindred closer together." He was not alone in this highly problematic belief. Many nineteenth-century thinkers, who had known the world of arranged marriages, believed that marriages based on choice and affection would be stronger than those based on economic considerations. Friedrich Engels made quite a point of this in his essay *The Origin of the Family, Private Property, and the State.* In their innocence, these early social theorists never considered that, along with choice in marriage, there might come the notion of choice correction, of periodically reviewing and possibly "upgrading the system," as we do with our computers and sound equipment.

Our American founders, too, seem to have taken the moral and intellectual state of the American people for granted. James Madison said as much in *Federalist No. 55*, where he wrote that republican government presupposes the existence of civic virtue to a greater degree than any other governmental form, and expressed his complete confidence that the "political character" and "the present genius" of the American people were equal to the challenge. This confident assumption by the Founders that our reserves of social capital were in excellent condition should not surprise us. Living in a country dotted with family farms and businesses, with most of the population clustered in tight-knit, self-governing communities, how could they have foreseen that individuals in the future would depend much less on their families—and more on their own wage labor or government—for social standing and economic security? How could they have anticipated the rise and decay of great cities (so despised by Thomas Jefferson)? Or the economic dependence of a great proportion of Americans on large public and private organizations? Or how much power these organizations would wield? The statesmen of our formative period left society to take care of itself, concentrated their energies on the laws, and produced a remarkable design for government. They believed their Constitution would show the world (as Alexander Hamilton wrote in *Federalist No. 1*) that human beings could establish good government by "reflection and choice," that the political destinies of men and women did not have to be controlled by force and accident. The Founders knew, to be sure, that a good legal framework—even the greatest one ever devised—was not enough. This is evident from the many allusions made by John Adams, Jefferson, and Madison to the importance of civic wisdom and virtue. But it seems not to have occurred to our early statesmen that the seedbeds of virtue would need tending. The social environment was just there, like the natural environment. In both respects we seemed endowed with inexhaustible riches.

What Tocqueville and the Founders were unable to foresee is now plain to everyone. But the first question they would have been likely to ask is the very one we avoid: What are the implications of present-day conditions of family life for the American experiment in ordered liberty? Let us try to think for a moment about what kinds of things we would notice if we looked at familiar demographic data, not primarily in terms of their psychological effects on individuals or their economic consequences for society, but from a political point of view. Consider, for example:

1. Parental employment outside the home. The separation of home and business has cut down on opportunities for family members to plan and carry out common projects. With fewer joint family activities, less time spent by parents with children, and less regular contact with other relatives, the opportunities for learning and observing elementary social skills are further reduced. Women are still the main teachers of children but their capabilities are stretched to their utter limits as they try to combine primary responsibility for child raising with responsibilities in the work force. The task of nurture is often shared with low-paid, poorly motivated baby-sitters, and the task of education is increasingly assumed by television and peers.

2. Birthrates. The fact that current birthrates are up among poor, unmarried teens and down among affluent,

educated elites is also of potentially far-reaching political importance. Among other things, it means that, increasingly, policymakers in this country are apt to be persons without children or persons who have children but seldom see them, while the nation's children are concentrated in lower-income households.

3. Families and their environments of other social groups. While families have been changing, the neighborhoods, churches, schools, and other networks of support around them have been changing too. Small, close-knit groups of interdependent people are the principal settings where we acquire the skills of participation, where we accumulate clear, practical ideas about the nature of our duties and the extent of our rights, and where each generation learns anew to appreciate the benefits and sacrifices necessary for a constitutional order. Yet local governments and intermediate groups of all sorts seem to be losing much of their vitality.

4. Poor, fatherless families. The ranks of poor, female-headed homes have been swelled by rises both in divorce and in births outside marriage. Since 1960, the proportion of children growing up without a father in the home has more than doubled; it now stands at about one in four. Whatever the benefits of divorce and the successes of single parenthood in individual cases, their current high incidence has produced a large proportion of children who live in poverty and who have never had the opportunity to learn what a father does. Psychologist Judith Wallerstein (who recently conducted the first long-term study of the effects of divorce on children) has found that "underachievement, drifting, a sense of deprivation, and psychological problems" endure among chil-

dren of divorced parents well into the third decade of life. These are not just problems of the families involved, she says. They affect all of us, sending out a "widespread, powerful ripple effect on the whole society."

As I have indicated, there is very little speculation among partisans in the war over the family about how these well-known phenomena may bear on the capacity for participation in civic life. But here and there some evidence is accumulating. One of the most interesting sources is a study conducted in 1989 by People for the American Way. Startled by its own findings, this civil rights advocacy group prefaced its report with the statement that it was time "to sound the alarm about the toll that the growing disconnectedness of America's young people will exact from our democracy." The survey showed that a sense of the importance of civic participation was almost entirely lacking in what it called "Democracy's Next Generation." On the basis of extensive interviews with American youths between the ages of 15 and 24, the study concluded that "young people have learned only half of America's story": They appreciate the democratic freedoms we enjoy but fail to perceive a need to recipro-cate by exercising the duties and responsibilities of good citizenship. The notion of freedom entertained by most of the young people, furthermore, had a disquieting re-semblance to what the classical philosophers would have called "license"—the pursuit of unlimited self-gratifi-cation. Though distressed enough to sound an alarm, People for the American Way did not once in its report suggest there might be any connection between the con-ditions under which American children are being raised and the political attitudes they exhibit.

In fact, one could read this report and conclude, as I suppose many people have done, that the attitudes it records are merely a function of immaturity and that members of the current generation are probably no more or less self-centered or politically apathetic than their parents once were. That comforting interpretation, however, was made less tenable by a second study (released in June 1990 by the Times Mirror Center), also reporting a widespread indifference among young adults toward government, politics, public affairs—and even toward news about the outside world. Unlike the first study, the Times Mirror report used fifty years of public opinion data to compare today's young people with young Americans of the past. The report concluded that the current group knows less, cares less, votes less, and is less critical of its leaders and institutions than young people at any time in the past several decades. The Times Mirror group found that "over most of the past five decades, younger members of the public have been at least as well informed as older people" but that with the current generation that is no longer the case. Without attempting to offer a full explanation of why this might be so, the group did speculate, almost offhandedly, that the "decline of the family" might be a possible part of the explanation.

Meanwhile, sociologists Alice and Peter Rossi of the University of Massachusetts have been investigating the possible sources of feelings of obligation. In an unpublished paper the Rossis have reported a strong correlation between the sense of obligation people report that they feel for their kinfolk and their sense of obligation to a wider community and society at large. They thus have provided some empirical support for Edmund Burke's famous observation that the seeds of public affection are in our attachment to our own "little platoons" in society.

Finally, on a more anecdotal level, Barbara White-head reports, on the basis of a series of public discussions organized by a newly-formed family advocacy group, that parents themselves say their number one concern is that they are failing in their efforts to pass on their own values to their children. Though financial strain and the problems of combining work and home life are high on their list, their main worry, they say, is the struggle for the hearts and minds of their children in an aggressively materialist culture. ("Reports from the Kitchen Table," *Family Affairs*, Vol. 3, No. 1 [1990].)

All these bits of evidence, I suggest, make the "war over the family" look less like a war and more like a game of blindman's buff. There are, no doubt, many reasons why public discourse fails to focus on the political di-mensions of such an important subject. Let me suggest three. One is the defect of our virtues. Two of the hall-marks of a liberal society are tolerance and broad-mindedness. Most of us take these obligations very seri-ously and thus find it hard to talk about matters that involve character. The same people who would decon-struct the family into meaninglessness have quite suc-cessfully promulgated the messages that virtue is a matter of personal taste or preference, that it is bad to feel guilty and even worse to be "judgmental." A second factor that makes this kind of discussion difficult is that many features of current patterns of family organization are associated with beneficial social developments. What do we do when major improvements in the educational and economic position of women, for example, are—or seem to be—in serious tension with optimal conditions for the raising of children? The third reason for our reticence that I would mention is the famous line from Pogo: "We have met the enemy and they is us." How many of us parents, if we are really honest, can say we have not passed the economic or emotional cost of some personal goal on to our children?

It is easier not to talk about such matters. But what if one *did* take seriously the mounting evidence that our "free society" has been living on inherited social capital for quite some time, consuming without replenishing many of the resources that have made possible "the orderly pursuit of happiness by free men and women"?

As an initial matter, it seems to me that we could do worse than to adopt the stance that men and women in Eastern Europe took in recent years as they mounted a struggle for freedom against mighty odds: namely, to begin to tell the truth about what is happening. As Timothy Garton Ash has reported, the principal slogans that animated the freedom movements all over East Central Europe in the 1980s had to do with "calling good and evil by name" and with "living in truth." (*The Uses of Adversity: Essays on the Fate of Central Europe*, Random House, 1989.) Individual men and women trying to "live in truth" began to come together in mutual aid associations, like Solidarity in Poland; in little groups in the basements of Lutheran churches in East Germany; in Civic Forum in Czechoslovakia; and in dozens of little societies that suddenly sprang to life in Hungary. According to Ash, these spontaneous movements in turn gave rise to another *leitmotif* of the pre-1989 period, the resurgence of "civil society." Civil society, in this sense, refers to the myriad grass-roots social structures within which we learn and practice the skills of government, the intermediate associations that stand between the individual and the centralized state, and the social networks that can support and share with families the task of educating and inspiring the next generation.

Telling the truth, or trying to find out what the truth is, of course, is only a beginning. But, on the hypothesis that America's child-raising environments and its political future may be strongly connected, let us now revisit the four positions that I outlined at the beginning of this lecture. I want to suggest that all of them are deeply flawed and that, in order to move from the war over the family to sitting down and reasoning together about the family, we need to reformulate the terms and reexamine the implicit premises of the entire debate.

Let us turn first to the quarrel over words: whether to refer to "families" or "the family." From the point of view of institutional analysis these terms are interchangeable, so long as it is understood that the family, as a social institution, takes many forms (like "the firm" in business, or "the law"). In a given society at a given time, a single family type may be so prevalent that people may speak of "the family" to designate that type. Anthropologists and sociologists usefully remind us, however, (1) that many family types coexist in every society but (2) that family forms are not infinitely various. Generally, social scientists reserve the term "family" for groups containing more than one generation.

The problem with much family discussion coming from the cultural right is that "the family" too often is understood as isomorphic with the homemaker-bread-winner unit. Far from being "traditional," the family type where all members depended on a male earner was not even possible for large numbers of people until the first part of this century. Previously, most men and women in America were economically *interdependent* in family farms or businesses. Now that women have followed men into the labor force, most families are interdependent once again, but both spouses are working outside the home. (The new interdependence is highly asymmetrical, however, a point to which I shall return.) At this point, what is important to notice is that today any program for family policy that takes sharp sex-role divisions in child raising and income production to be normative leaves most American families out of the picture. In view of changes in women's aspirations, of the high risk of divorce, and of the economic pressures that bear down especially hard on child-raising households, it is unlikely that the breadwinner-homemaker model will have a strong resurgence in the foreseeable future. What we do see, however, is the use of that model for a period of time when children are small, with all the risks borne by the parent who stays at home.

The positions that are characteristic of family discussion on the cultural left are equally out of touch with everyday life, for the idea that gender-related differences in child-raising roles and income production will disappear anytime soon is also unrealistic. Furthermore, the idea of family members as separate and independent of one another is as much at variance with actual American family behavior as the old single-earner family model has become. If any family model is typical now, it is one where both parents are employed but where the wife's employment yields lower pay, lower status, and less security than the husband's.

Now let us consider the second point of view that often informs perceptions of family life on the cultural left. This is the notion that a "family" is whatever one wants it to be—a group of roommates, a homosexual couple, an elderly invalid living with a caretaker, and so on. This project of "deconstruction" is deployed in the service of various aims, some related to gaining equal access to "family" benefits and some aimed at securing legitimation of life-styles that have traditionally been socially disapproved. Here it seems to me that the path of prudence requires rejecting the notion that "family" has to have the same definition in all contexts. Much depends on the purpose of the rules or programs involved. For many purposes it will make sense to follow the lead of other liberal democracies that make a distinction between households that are engaged in child raising and those involving other types of living arrangements. It seems fairly clear that we all have a much greater interest in the circumstances under which children are being raised than we do in the way that adults choose to arrange their lives. Thus it seems appropriate for society and government to accord special treatment to those engaged in child raising and to seek in every way possible to promote and reinforce parental responsibility. Singling out the category of child-raising households for certain purposes does not belittle or degrade childless individuals. It merely recognizes the special needs of child-raising units and the high public interest in the nurture and education of future citizens.

When we turn to the question of *how* to aid child-raising families, we find ourselves in the midst of the battle between the economic right and left. There, many in both camps now agree that we must vigorously enforce the child-support laws, but beyond this there is little common ground. The economic left often advocates that government should come to the aid of families with massive public day-care, educational, and financial assistance programs, while the economic right insists that there's nothing like good old private enterprise and self-reliance. Fortunately, however, the choices need not be limited to those between direct government provision of services and radical laissez-faire. Even the North European welfare states have begun to recognize, now that they are running up against economic limits, that small nongovernmental groups often can deliver social services such as education, child care, and care for the infirm better and more efficiently than the state.

Consider, for example, various possible alternative approaches to the problem of providing day care for preschool children. At present in the United States, government has remained largely aloof. This gives us a pretty good idea of what is yielded by the hands-off approach favored by many conservatives: Too much day care is being provided by poorly qualified persons for whom it is just another minimum-wage job, and too many children are simply left alone while the parent or parents are at work. Yet, if the only alternative is to turn preschoolers over to the same people who have presided over the decline of the public schools, we seem to be caught between a rock and a hard place. Somewhat more promising is the appearance here and there of day-care centers at the parents' workplaces, as part of employer awareness of what is required to attract and keep good employees. More promising still might be the adoption of measures that would make it easier for a parent to remain at home for the crucial first year or two after a child is born, as many European countries have done. Other approaches that should be encouraged include day care provided by parishes and temples, where it would serve the triple purpose of providing meaningful work for members of the community (especially older people), of responding to a pressing need of the community's young couples, and of beginning the religious education of the community's children. The 1990 child-care legislation takes a few steps forward by recognizing that government need not be a provider in order to be a supporter of day care by persons who are well qualified and highly motivated.

The really difficult problems, of course, concern how to judge when families would benefit most from a hands-off approach, when direct government aid would be advisable, or when more indirect types of public assistance would be most beneficial. The fact is that we really do not know very much about how to support, or how to reinforce, or even how to avoid harm to ongoing, mutually conditioning systems like families, neighborhoods, and their related institutions. Here, therefore, I believe we would do well to take a leaf from the books of some of the most creative contemporary thinkers in the social sciences. Psychologist Urie Bronfenbrenner, anthropologist Clifford Geertz, and sociologist Robert Bellah all use the term "ecological" to describe the kind of approach that is needed when we are dealing with ongoing social systems. The term seems to me to be appropriate because the problems of protecting social environments like families and their surrounding institutions are in many ways comparable to those of safeguarding natural environments.

If democratic states need individual citizens with an array of qualities that—so far as we know—can best be nurtured within interactive and reasonably stable families; if families, in order to function effectively, need to be composed of individuals capable of commitment and supported by communities of various sorts; and if the health of communities in turn depends on certain kinds of individuals and families, an ecological perspective is essential. The basic problem is one of setting conditions or, to put it another way, of shifting probabilities. For us specific-target-oriented Americans, this will be quite a mental shift.

What little we know about how law affects and is affected by other social subsystems and by the culture as a whole suggests that we should not hold exaggerated expectations of what law and government can accomplish on their own. But there are a number of ways in which law and government—following an ecological approach— might try to be helpful in setting better conditions for child-raising families. They could at least endeavor to support (or not to undermine) the values of commitment and responsibility; to support (or to avoid harm to) the social structures on which families rely; and to surmount the present-mindedness that characterizes so much of our public policymaking. Recognizing the primitive state of our knowledge about the likely long-term effects of changes in these areas, an ecological approach to family policy should proceed modestly, preferring local experiments to broad standardized programs and avoiding court-imposed uniformity by excessive "constitutionalization" of family issues.

With these general principles in mind, let me try to be somewhat more specific, beginning with the idea of reinforcing, or at least trying not to undermine, the efforts of men and women who are doing their best, day in and day out, to raise their children to lead personally satisfying and socially productive lives. At the top of the list, we ought to avoid giving the appearance of indifference to these efforts. That is, we should not treat dedication to child raising as though it were just one more "life-style" about which the state must be "neutral." A close second (and second only because we have already begun to move in this direction) is avoiding the appearance of sanctioning parental irresponsibility (as we did for so long in the area of child support).

At a practical level, now that the two-earner child-raising household has become typical, employers and unions must adapt to the fact that most employees, male and female, have family roles in addition to their work roles. Government must give more attention to the likely impact of tax, employment, and social assistance laws and policies on families. We urgently need to consider how government and employers can assist men and women in carrying out the family responsibilities that most of them bear; how men can be persuaded to share with women more of the double burden of wage work and home work; and how family members who perform caretaking roles can be protected from the risks entailed by their asymmetrical dependence on the principal family earner. At a minimum, we must be attentive to the ways in which governmental or employer policies may inadvertently be discouraging, impeding, or even penalizing those who are responsibly trying to carry out family roles. We should not have to apologize for defining our society as one that relies heavily on families to socialize its future citizens and that encourages, aids, and rewards persons who perform family obligations.

Another indispensable element of an effort to set conditions for the nurture of citizens is to attend more closely to the health of the social structures with which families are in a symbiotic relationship—neighborhoods, churches, schools, and voluntary associations. It is, of course, difficult to determine just how law and policy might help to revitalize or even to refrain from harming these fragile structures. Yet, what we lose as these little groups seemingly recede before the advance of the state, the market, and the "culture of narcissism" is far from negligible.

The shift to an ecological perspective such as the one I have been advocating inevitably raises the key ecological question: Is the damage with which we are concerned here irreversible? I have been counseling an approach to social and legal family policy that would combine many concerns of both progressives and conservatives, that would work patiently toward long-range goals, and that would seek to promote the general welfare by attending to the conditions under which individuals, families, and communities prosper. Like the analogous problems of protecting the air and water, this approach would require both a certain sense of the long run and a certain willingness to sacrifice, neither of which is easy to marshal in modern society. As in the case of natural ecological systems, the possibility exists that the task is beyond the capacity of law and government to affect for the better. If, in fact, our societies are producing too many individuals who are capable neither of effective participation in civic life nor of sustaining personal relationships, it is probably not within our power to reverse the process.

Nathan Glazer has recently written:

> "[There is much to be said both] for the insistence on a radical and egalitarian individualism, and for the defense of complex institutions and social bonds.... But if the first side wins out, as it is doing, the hope that social policy will assist in creating more harmonious social relations, better-working social institutions broadly accepted as the decent and right way to order society, cannot be realized." (*The Limits of Social Policy*, Harvard University Press, 1988, p. 155.)

It may be, however, that one reason that "radical and egalitarian individualism" often appears to be "winning out" is that it so thoroughly permeates the mass media and the legal system. I suspect, however, that the individualism of the knowledge class and of the entertainment industry is more thoroughgoing than that which exists in our culture generally. Though Robert Bellah and his coauthors of *Habits of the Heart* found that the "first language" of Americans is the discourse of individualism, they also heard Americans across the country speaking communitarian "second languages," languages of "tradition and commitment in communities of memory." It is true that individuals in modern societies have been emancipated from group and family ties to a historically unprecedented degree, but as Michael Walzer has written, we have not yet reached the point where we are all isolated monads:

> "[C]ommunal feeling and belief seem considerably more stable than we once thought they would be, and the proliferation of secondary associations in liberal society is remarkable—even if many of them have short lives and transient memberships. One has the sense of people working together and trying to cope, and not . . . just getting by on their own, by themselves, one by one." ("The Communitarian Critique of Liberalism," *Political Theory*, Vol. 18, No. 1, pp. 11–12 [February 1990].)

One might add to Walzer's observation that these same Americans who still join voluntary associations continue to still spend most of their lives in emotionally and economically interdependent households. And the majority of the same young people whom the polls show to be apathetic about public life state that they look forward to raising children within a lasting, monogamous, heterosexual relationship. It may be, as sociologist David Popenoe has said, that, "the longer that individualist (me) values are at the fore, the more people realize that social (family) values are seriously lacking." Perhaps, as he optimistically suggests, the 1990s will bring the demise of the "me generation." ("Family Decline in America," in *Rebuilding the Nest*, ed. David Blankenhorn, Family Service America, 1990, p. 39.)

Only time will tell whether this is so. It is both encouraging and sobering to remember in this connection, how-

ever, that a great many members of what has been called
the "me generation" never did participate fully in its
values. I am referring to many of its young women.
Tocqueville once gave us a memorable verbal portrait of
the American women of the frontier. He was perceptive
enough to recognize not only the strength but the sadness
of these women:

> "In the utmost confines of the wilderness I have often
> met young wives, brought up in all the refinements of
> life in the towns of New England, who have passed
> almost without transition from their parents' pros-
> perous houses to leaky cabins in the depths of the
> forest. Fever, solitude, and boredom had not broken
> the resilience of their courage. Their features were
> changed and faded, but their looks were firm. They
> seemed both sad and resolute."

If we look around us today, I believe we see a similar
strength and sadness in American women who are raising families, or who have raised families, under new conditions. The current generation of women has had its
own frontier—the unknown territory created by unprecedented changes in sexual behavior and in understandings about gender roles and family life. Knowing
full well where their self-interest (in a purely economic
sense) lies, and given the birth-control technology and
unprecedented opportunity to pursue that self-interest,
they overwhelmingly still choose motherhood with its
attendant risks. In marriage, they accept primary responsibility for child care, thereby incurring disadvan-
tages in the labor force. Upon divorce, they seek and

accept child custody, even though they are not well
equipped to deal with it financially. This behavior may
support Tocqueville's belief that there are some natural
ties, after all, that are stronger than legal or social ties.
However that may be, it seems to me no less true today
than in Jacksonian America that our experiment in government depends more on the mores than on the law and
that the moral and intellectual climate for children is
still chiefly shaped by American women. Whether the
lives of these women will be spent in a modern wilder-
ness rushing, exhausted, from job to home, underpaid
and undervalued in the former and unaided or abandoned in the latter, we do not know. If that is to be their
situation, then, like their forebears, sad and resolute,
they will do what they have to do. At present, however,
for too many of them, the daily struggle for existence
keeps them from providing their children with the
essentials for human development. How we as a society
now respond to their circumstances will determine,
more than anything else, "the meaning of the family in a
free society."

AMERICAN FAMILIES: HOW DO WE PICK UP THE PIECES?

by

Madeleine M. Kunin

Madeleine M. Kunin

Madeleine M. Kunin was elected to a third term as Governor of Vermont on November 8, 1988. She became Vermont's seventy-fourth Governor in January 1985 and is the first woman in U.S. history to be elected Governor three times.

She was born in Zurich, Switzerland and immigrated to the United States in 1940. Governor Kunin earned a B.A. degree in history from the University of Massachusetts in 1956, an M.A. degree in journalism from Columbia University, and an M.A. degree in English literature from the University of Vermont. In addition, she has been awarded numerous honorary degrees. She has been a fellow at Harvard University's Institute of Politics at the Kennedy School of Government and has taught at Middlebury College and St. Michael's College.

In 1972, Governor Kunin won her first political election, to a seat in the Vermont House of Representatives. She served three two-year terms, was elected Democratic Whip in her second term, and chaired the House Appropriations Committee in 1977-78. Governor Kunin was elected Lieutenant Governor of Vermont in 1978 and won re-election in 1980.

During her tenure, Governor Kunin scored significant achievements in the areas of the environment, education, and the economy. Fortune magazine named her as one of the country's ten education governors. In addition, Vermont was cited by the Children's Defense Fund as having the best health, education, and social service programs for children and by the Institute for Southern Studies as the number one state for its efforts to protect the environment.

Governor Kunin made Vermont a national leader in child care services, initiating a cooperative effort between the public and private sectors to promote and establish child care facilities across Vermont.

AMERICAN FAMILIES: HOW DO WE
PICK UP THE PIECES?

by

Madeleine M. Kunin

All governors have a keen interest in the well-being of families, because governors know that here we face the most fundamental test of our effectiveness. If we fail to strengthen our states' families, we are doomed to reap a bitter harvest of poverty in years to come, resulting in an uneducated and unskilled work force, as well as new waves of crime and violence. Governors concerned about improving the standard of living, as well as the quality of life, of their citizens have little choice: We are compelled to address family needs for both economic and humanitarian reasons. Regardless of party or political ideology, governors widely share this conclusion, and we have done so earlier and more avidly than political leaders in Washington.

Before I elaborate on that statement, however, I would like to acknowledge that even as we recognize the obvious—that healthy families lead to a healthy economy— we still don't know precisely how best to achieve the goal of fostering healthy families. Many questions concern us, and I will discuss some of them with you here:

1. The states have forged ahead of the federal government with innovative social programs to support the family, but how do we create nationwide equal opportunities for all Americans?

85

2. How do the states pay for social programs when the federal government continues to fund less and demand more, while beating the partisan drum of "no new taxes"?

3. How do we define the proper relationship of government, whether state or federal, to the family?

4. What is the appropriate relationship of the employer, the private sector, to family policy and decisions?

5. Finally, is there something else that has little to do with government and more to do with moral and spiritual values that contributes to the disintegration of the social fabric, and if so, how do we address issues such as honesty, commitment, and responsibility?

Let us return to the observation that it has been the governors of this country who, in recent years, have been leaders on family issues. It was Bill Clinton, a Democrat from Arkansas, and Michael Castle, a Republican from Delaware, who led the fight for welfare reform on behalf of the other governors. And it was a bipartisan group of governors, led by Roy Roemer of Colorado and Carroll Campbell of South Carolina, who engaged the President in education restructuring and goal setting.

We must remember that the governors called for reform while Ronald Reagan was still telling stories about welfare queens walking up to the checkout counter to buy vodka with food stamps. I was in the East Room of the White House with the National Governors Association when he did so. Ronald Reagan reflected the common assumption, which prevailed for many years in this country, equating "welfare reform" with "getting the cheats off welfare."

I remember my chagrin when I campaigned for my first statewide office in 1978 in St. Albans, Vermont, and was interviewed on a call-in talk show. The host was a conservative young man who knew how to attract the anti-welfare crowd. One after another they called in, railing against the cheaters, but my host topped them all when he referred to welfare mothers as "professional breeders."

Happily, most governors do not talk or think that way. Neither do most of the rest of us. One reason they do not is that we know that simply getting people off welfare is not enough. First of all, they come right back on again, and, second, in today's world nobody can support a family by simply doing "an honest day's work," if by that you mean unskilled physical labor such as pushing a broom, cutting wood, or using a pick and shovel.

That is why governors in many states began to approach welfare reform by asking a very different question. We asked, how can we enable our citizens to become self-supporting, not just for a couple of months, or even a year, but for the rest of their working lives? No longer was this a debate between hard-nosed Republican conservatives and bleeding-heart Democratic liberals, as my radio station host had framed it. Instead, both liberals and conservatives formed a new coalition, combining compassion with economic necessity. We knew we could not attract good jobs at good pay to our states, or keep them there, if we had a work force incapable of working. Fortunately, we had an ally in the wings—

American business—that agreed we could not continue to "waste" millions of Americans.

Together we asked, what are the obstacles that stand in the way of economic independence for welfare recipients? We found the answers to be lack of education, lack of child care, lack of health care. These are the things we began to provide because we understood that most of our welfare population was not cheating—these people had been cheated of a basic education and skills they needed to hold a job that paid a living wage.

I saw that with my own eyes as Governor of Vermont, and so I initiated our welfare reform program. When I was first elected six years ago, I was determined to improve the lives of Vermont's families and children. My prime responsibility was to raise our living standard. I was haunted by the faces I had seen during the campaign, the women doing piecework in the sewing factories, the faces in the crowd along the Fourth of July parade route.

Parades are instructive, if you know where to look. Walking past some houses, it was easy to smile and wave. These were the houses with pretty geraniums in the flower boxes, neatly trimmed lawns, and the intact three-generation extended family all spread out by the curb, comfortable in their lawn chairs. But in another part of town, it was different. Up on the second floor on a sagging paint-peeling balcony, men and women crowded together, looking down at the parade. Standing somewhat apart was a young girl who looked no more than twelve years old, holding her arms straight out as if she were carrying a tray, and in those arms was a tiny baby, covered with a graying blanket that had once been white.

Further on, a family was sitting on a pink chenille bed-spread in the back of a pickup truck, the children pale and listless, the mothers overweight and impatient with their kids. What I saw, I knew, were the signs and symptoms of poverty.

These were the signs I wanted to erase as governor. I began by bringing together three groups of government bureaucracy that had always operated apart from one another: employment and training, social welfare, and education. Fortunately, the commissioners of two of these agencies were my new appointees, and they were ready to break down turf boundaries and work together.

The result was a program called Reach Up. Its philosophy is simply stated:

> "Families on welfare want a better life than welfare can provide. Because many parents receiving Aid to Needy Families with Children have limited skills, work experience and education, they find that good jobs, those with decent wages, health benefits and security, are not within their grasp. Reach Up offers ANFC parents the opportunity of financial help, education, job training and support services to help them overcome these barriers. The aim of Reach Up is to prevent continued welfare dependency, to prepare people to succeed in the labor force, thus enabling families to achieve long-term independence from welfare." (Summary of Vermont Reach Up Program, Veronica Celani, Commissioner of Social Welfare.)

An example of one innovative Reach Up program is Community Service Scholars. The program allows single parents to attend college without expense, in conjunction with volunteer work in a service organization linked to the students' field of study. One advantage of this approach is that students immediately find themselves in occupationally oriented studies. The data prove that the program is succeeding, although we would like wage levels to rise even faster. Eighty percent of the participants are single parents, women who never finished high school or worked outside the home.

The individual success stories are very moving. The women and men who are in the Reach Up program exude an extraordinary pride. One woman came up to me the other evening to say, "Thank you for the Reach Up program. I'm going to Castleton State College. My kids are so proud of me. It has changed my life." That is what welfare reform is about—changing lives, giving new hope to people who had almost lost hope.

In conjunction with this welfare reform program, we in Vermont have made a major investment in child care, providing subsidized care to an increasingly larger population in response to the growing number of women in the work force. Undoubtedly you are familiar with the statistics of this story. In 1950, 12 percent of the women in the United States with children under six were in the paid labor force. By 1988, 57 percent were working. Vermont has historically had even higher participation. For women over sixteen, 63.7 percent were in the work force in 1989, the second highest percentage in the nation.

In response to the changing family, the number of children receiving subsidized child care has multiplied almost four times since I have been governor. This subsidy has been a major financial investment.

Vermont has taken further steps to strengthen families. In 1990 we established a family court, which enables us to combine all family matters—divorce, domestic abuse, child support, parentage, juvenile, mental health, and protective services cases—in one jurisdiction. This court will be less adversarial in nature and more supportive of families in distress.

In tandem with the establishment of this new judicial system, we enacted a tough wage-withholding law to ensure child support payments. Together these two steps will have a dramatic effect on the standard of living of the children of divorce and separation, many of whom now are relegated to poverty solely because of the inability of mothers to collect support payments. (A study of child support in Vermont had shown that one-third of all children were eligible for child support and that 39 percent of the parents of those children did not have legal orders requiring the absent parent to pay. Of those with such orders, only half were receiving full payment. These were the conditions that the new laws were designed to remedy.)

In addition to taking these remedial steps to rebuild families that have been impoverished, often both economically and emotionally, Vermont, like many other states, has made a strong investment in prevention, hoping to reverse cycles of deprivation. It was recently named the number one state in the nation in two key areas: services for children, by the Children's Defense Fund, and mental health services, in the Torrey Report by the National Alliance for the Mentally Ill. We have invested heavily in social service in Vermont. One indicator of our commitment is the payment we make to needy families with children. Vermont ranks third, following Alaska and California, in the level of its support payments. (For example, in Vermont a family of three receives $630 a month from the state, plus an additional amount from the county—$679 a month in Chittenden County. In Texas, by way of comparison, such a family would receive $184 a month if one parent is in residence or $200 a month if two are in residence.)

All of these initiatives indicate that during the Reagan years, when the federal government pulled back from social programs, the states stepped in to fill part of the gap. The good news is that programs like Reach Up in Vermont and their equivalents in Massachusetts, Delaware, Missouri, and other states have enabled many families to get back on their feet and discover long-term economic self-sufficiency. There is no doubt that with the elimination of poverty, many other problems, such as family violence and malnutrition, are also eliminated.

The bad news is that access to these programs and services depends on where in the United States you happen to live. In the last few years, the federal government and the states have reversed their roles of responsibility for domestic policy. In the 1950s, 1960s, and even 1970s, the federal government, using the carrot and the stick, saw to it that the states met a higher and more uniform standard. That was the case with civil rights and with early social service policies, such as welfare. Today, it is the states that are raising the standards, and these innovations have been creative, reflecting local priorities. But with that role reversal, we are also seeing great variation from state to state.

The fundamental question remains, how do we create

equal opportunity for American families, particularly at
a time when the number of children living in poverty continues to be more than 20 percent for all children and 49
percent for black children under the age of six. (Harry
D. Krause, "Child Support Reassessed," *Family Law
Quarterly*, Vol. XXIV, No. 1, Spring 1990, p. 15.)

Two problems stand in the way of equity. One is where
the political clout is, and the other, where the money is.
To some extent, they are one and the same.

This country is a generous country for those in need,
but it is much more generous to the needy elderly than to
the needy young. In the 1980s the incomes of elderly
Americans rose 16 percent, while the incomes of other
Americans stayed the same or were reduced. (*Ibid.*) The
power of the senior citizen lobby was demonstrated by
the rejection of the first recent deficit reduction and tax
package by the Congress. The largest outcry came as a
result of the increased Medicare payments. Seniors spoke
out and won. About a year ago a similar scenario was
played out when middle- and upper-income elderly Americans succeeded in repealing catastrophic health insurance.

On the other hand, the lack of political clout on the part
of dependent children and their caretakers was demonstrated when the President vetoed the Family Leave bill
in the fall of 1990 without suffering any perceptible political damage. When women and children are in need,
the perception persists that it is the victim's fault, and
there is insufficient realization that poor families are
largely created by the desertion of male support. If we
are to maintain and increase family support programs
such as child care, prenatal health care, and welfare re-

form, we must develop a better strategy to mobilize the political power structure of this country on behalf of our children. Organizations such as the Children's Defense Fund are leading a noble battle, and Marion Wright Edelman, its chair, is one of the heroines of our time. But she cannot wage this battle alone.

We have to acknowledge that these programs, which prevent family breakdown and help broken families mend themselves, cannot survive without adequate funding. If that requires taxes, then a bipartisan effort must acknowledge this reality.

The shift in responsibility from the federal government to the states has resulted in a parellel shift of financial responsibility. In the 1990 election, six incumbent governors were defeated, and several of those losses are attributed to the fact that the governors had to raise taxes. States cannot play the smoke and mirror deficit games that the federal government has perfected. Neither can we abandon our responsibilities to those in our midst who are most vulnerable.

In good times, when the economy is expanding, states can be responsive to growing needs without raising taxes. We in Vermont have been. But in an economic downturn, such as we are experiencing in the Northeast and you experienced recently in Texas, it is impossible to be responsible without tax increases.

I believe we must stop fooling the American people into believing that they can have everything they expect from government without making any personal sacrifice. We cannot let them believe that they can ignore the children of this generation without paying a very heavy price in increased violence and reduced productivity in the next generation. Already in urban areas such as New York, one in four young black men is either in jail or on probation—an extraordinarily depressing statistic that is undoubtedly a consequence of generations of poverty and social breakdown.

If we are to make a strong political and financial commitment, we must also clarify what role the private sector, parents, and government should play in the life of the family. I believe it is time that we establish strong linkages, as well as clear lines of responsibility, among all three.

Today, one reason for the breakdown of families is that no one takes responsibility for the lives of the children who are left without hearth, home, love, or care. Primary responsibility, naturally, rests with the parents, but since women frequently are either key cosupporters in two-parent families or the sole support in single-parent families, it is critically necessary to open channels between employers and working parents.

In my state, I am delighted to say, we have a maternal leave policy, 45 firms have on-site or near-site child care facilities, and more than 50 companies offer child care subsidies, vouchers, or dependent care assistance plans. The benefits of such programs are a pleasure to describe. In a nationwide study of 415 firms offering child care benefits, these results occurred:

Reduced turnover—65 percent

Increased recruitment—85 percent

Improved morale—90 percent

Reduced absenteeism—53 percent

Policies such as flexible work schedules, family leave policies, and job sharing will have to become commonplace if working families are to meet their dual responsibilities of providing both economic and emotional security to their children. The private sector must increasingly take the lead, rather than being cajoled or forced into this new role, because it is in corporate America's self-interest to acknowledge and support the needs of the changing American family. That is the only road to increased productivity and competitiveness and to a more humane society.

But when I look at the statistics that indicate the level of wear and tear on the American family—the number of teenage parents, the number of children in jail, the number of babies dying in infancy, the level of drug addiction—I believe there is something else happening in our society that we do not fully understand. The very social fabric, which used to be sustained by religion, by tradition, is frayed. In recent years, we developed a permissive attitude toward parents themselves, exemplified by a court decision that concludes, "[T]here are divergent views, at law and in equity, as to the fundamental nature of a parent's obligation to maintain an infant child . . ." (*Id.*, p. 5.)

As early as the common law of the 1750s, Blackstone made it clear that "the duty of parents to provide for the maintenance of their children is a principle of natural law. . . . By begetting them, therefore, they have entered into a voluntary obligation, to endeavor, as far as in them lies, that the life which they have bestowed shall be supported and preserved." (*Id.*, p. 6.) This is the moral and ethical principle that we must articulate with renewed vigor and that must be reflected in our laws, as well as in our social attitudes. This is the firm principle behind our tougher child support laws, which make it clear that if you father a child, you cannot walk away, you are responsible for the life of that child, regardless of whether or not you become the husband of the child's mother.

To get that message across, we must begin to address the needs and responsibilities of young fathers with the same intensity that we have focused on young mothers. We could have a major impact on the emotional and economic well-being of children if they could have the love and care of two parents, instead of being dependent exclusively on one, particularly when that parent is likewise a child. An example of what might be accomplished is a new program started for teenage dads in a parent/child center in Addison County, Vermont, an area with the lowest teenage pregnancy rate in the state. The Dads Program is for boys sixteen to twenty. They spend part of the week learning basic skills in the vocational education center, part of the time at work, and two days a week in the child care center. At first, the boys did not want to work in the day care room. "No way," Cheryl Mitchell, the director, told me. They started one afternoon a week and soon asked if they could be there two afternoons. Then they wanted to be there by themselves, so they could have sole responsibility for their babies. Many felt that because they could not support their babies, they did not have a right to be with them, and this program has permitted them to become fathers. It was frustrating for them not to be a part of their child's life, but they did not know how, because none of them had role models of responsible fathers in their own families.

Through this program, value messages are getting articulated. The major one is, if you get a girl pregnant, you are responsible for the baby. In addition, because many of these teenage fathers have already parented two or three children with different women, messages about birth control are also being emphasized.

I believe it is critical that, on the issue of responsible sexuality, we face up to reality. The statistics of teenage pregnancy in the United States, compared to those of other industrialized countries, are shocking. These statistics are unrelated to the level of teenage sexuality, which is approximately the same today everywhere. In 1988, in the United States, 96 teenagers per thousand became pregnant, while in England, the rate was 45 per thousand; in Canada, 44; and in the Netherlands, as low as 14. The key difference between the United States and these countries is birth-control counseling. If we could reduce unwanted teenage pregnancies in the United States to approximately a 4 percent level, equal to that of our neighbors, it is estimated that we would see a savings of $8.6 billion annually in this country. (Center for Population Options, Washington, D.C.) In Vermont, through our Teenage Pregnancy Task Force, we are beginning to make inroads in reducing unwanted pregnancies and making certain that teenage mothers receive proper prenatal care and birth-control information.

As we look at the American family today, we know it is a very different family than it used to be—the cover of the *Saturday Evening Post* showing Mom and Dad with a son and a daughter is as outdated as the magazine itself. But what has not changed is the fact that parents still want the very best for their children, and each generation looks at its children as the great new hope for a better future. What we must do as a society is not disappoint those children's or those parents' expectations. To succeed we must commit ourselves to an ambitious agenda for children, equal to the one we have put in place for the elderly. Just as Americans should not have to leave this world in fear and insecurity, our babies should not enter this world handicapped by poor prenatal care, drug addiction, and fear.

We must squarely face up to the fact that we have to pay for child care, for health care, and for education and that it is a small price to pay in comparison to what we are investing today, with almost no debate, in correctional facilities and other remedial institutions.

Finally, it is time to recognize that the best way to strengthen families is to establish responsibility for our children—the responsibility of both parents, the responsibility of employers, and the responsibility of government, when all else fails. This shared responsibility will help give our children a sense of values, of right and wrong, of belonging in a time and place, and of being wanted and loved. That is the best way I know to create happy and healthy families and, simultaneously, a great nation.

THE ROLE OF WOMEN IN THE WORK FORCE AND ITS IMPACT ON FAMILY LIFE

by

Rosemary M. Collyer

Rosemary M. Collyer

Rosemary M. Collyer is a Partner with the law firm of Crowell & Moring in Washington, D.C. She represents management clients in labor and employment law counseling and litigation. Prior to joining Crowell & Moring, Ms. Collyer was appointed by former President Ronald Reagan to serve as General Counsel of the National Labor Relations Board (1984–89). Ms. Collyer was previously appointed by President Reagan to serve as Chairman of the Federal Mine Safety and Health Review Commission (1981–84).

Ms. Collyer was an attorney with the law firm of Sherman & Howard in Denver, Colorado, before her government service. She graduated with honors from Trinity College, Washington, D.C., in 1968 and with honors from the University of Denver College of Law in 1977, where she was a member of the Law Review.

THE ROLE OF WOMEN IN THE WORK FORCE AND ITS IMPACT ON FAMILY LIFE

by

Rosemary M. Collyer*

Dr. Andrew R. Cecil has proved again that he is attuned to the heartbeat of America. No less an arbiter of Americana than *Time* magazine has devoted a special Fall 1990 issue to "Women: The Road Ahead." Obviously, *Time*'s editors must be looking at the focus of these lectures in determining the concerns of the country!

But Dr. Cecil requires us to be more thoughtful than the editors of a weekly magazine. Our charge is not just to consider what is happening with women, men, and their families, and why those things are happening, but also to address the impact of change on the moral values of a free society. Moral values are particularly hard to contemplate in the evolving free society of the United States at the end of the twentieth century. Our collective emphasis for over 200 years on individual freedoms has had the effect of depleting our sense of shared values: When we speak of "moral" values, whose values do we mean? The current, wrenching debate over abortion demonstrates the problem: Is abortion a civil rights issue with discriminatory undertones or is it, rather, a moral and religious question that must be answered "NO" in

---

*Mrs. Collyer would like to thank Victoria L. Eastus, an associate with Crowell & Moring, for her contributions to this paper.

order not to devalue children and life itself? Whenever we speak of moral values, we must remember that, to a great extent, our values do not coincide and that one of the greatest values of a free society is to allow different people to be different.

Within the context of a diverse society with diverse goals, my topic, "The Role of Women in the Work Force and Its Impact on Family Life," poses special difficulties for intelligent communication. This country needs women in its work force, but that fact does not solve the social and logistical dislocation caused by forging a new concept of the role of women. Each of you will hear this lecture within the contexts of your own experiences and opinions, which are almost certainly not all shared by all the others in this room, much less all of America.

I think I was asked to address this topic because in many ways I personify the "first wave" of the large-scale movement of working mothers into the labor force. The differences between my life and my mother's exemplify the changes in this country in less than a generation. My mother, who has all the intellect, drive, and capacity of any titan of industry, married early and raised nine children. Unlike her, ALL of us, whether male or female, work "outside the home." The changing times became obvious when, at age 29 and pregnant with my first child, I was accepted into law school. My mother's only fear was that I would *not* go on to school because of my son's birth. Unlike me, she had absolutely no doubts as to whether I should try to juggle both family and professional career.

Sixteen years ago, when Tim was born, I really believed it was possible to be a superwoman, to "have it all" without much difficulty beyond the logistics of child care. Now I know that the fact that I want to have a professional career has had subtle and not-so-subtle effects on my family. We are forced to make family choices every day that are different in kind and impact from the choices I had anticipated as I was growing up or the choices my mother made. One instance is, of course, that I am here in Dallas and my family remains in Washington, D.C., attending to family life without me! There are others, with much deeper meaning, that confront us regularly.

In 1935, Margaret Mead remarked that a woman had two choices. Either she proclaimed herself "a woman and therefore less an achieving individual, or an achieving individual and therefore less a woman." The woman who chose the first option increased her opportunity of being "a loved object, the kind of girl whom men will woo and boast of, toast and marry," while the woman who had hopes of achievements lost "her chance for the kind of love she wants." (Margaret Mead, "Sex and Achievement," *Forum*, November 1935, pp. 301–303, quoted in William H. Chafe, *The American Woman: Her Changing Social, Economic and Political Roles 1920–1970*, Oxford University Press, 1972, p. 100.)

These two choices, however limited and limiting they were in 1935, are no longer available to most American women. Like it or not, women work because they have to. Declining numbers of Harriets can afford to wait at home for their Ozzies to arrive. Harriet works because work defines people in the United States, because Harriet wants to share the satisfaction of job and status, because Harriet needs to contribute to the education of her children and protect her senior years, and, most of all, because her family relies on her income. Fully 85 percent of today's students think that there will be more divorces in the future than there have been in the past. ("The Dream of Youth," *Time*, Special Issue, Fall 1990, p. 14.) Tomorrow's Harriets will work too, and many will join the swelling ranks of single parents on whom all of the family burdens fall.

If the issues of concern to working women were merely work related, the solutions would be easier to identify and implement. It is ironic that one month before its special issue on women, *Time* ran a cover article titled "Do We Care About Our Kids? The sorry plight of America's most disadvantaged minority: its children." (*Time*, October 8, 1990.) For a variety of reasons ranging from innate biology to societal notions of a woman's proper role, the job of raising children has fallen mostly to women. Women have long had the primary responsibility for the care, shelter, feeding, clothing, and education of children. Most important, women as primary caregivers have had the main responsibility for the moral development of children. Fathers have always played important roles in training and disciplining children; nowadays many dads also provide the nurturing that we traditionally associate with mothers. However, a critical by-product of the movement of women into the day-to-day work force is the difficulty of maintaining a supportive family environment for children who see their parents only at the stressful times of early morning departure and exhausted evening meal preparation.

As America has moved work into factories and office buildings, family life and work life have ceased to be connected in time or space. Mothers have worked at the family business for generations, but that business centered around the home, whether on the farm, in the store under a flat, or in a plant in a relatively small town where every one knew everyone else and generations lived together. "Home and its surrounding community used to be everybody's operating base, with work and play and family pretty much intermixed," says Penelope Leach, author of a popular parenting manual. Now that that is no longer the case, home is described by *Time* as "little more than a dormitory." ("The Great Experiment," *Time*, Special Issue, Fall 1990.)

There *are* instances when the two intersect. Working in my office on a weekend, I encounter a colleague who is racing her young daughter to the rest room. Mother is working on Saturday and her daughter is still in the process of potty training. How much legal work will be accomplished remains to be seen! When I comment on "doing it all at once," this mother retorts, "I'm not trying to be superwoman. I'm just trying to pay the mortgage." It is these occasions that working women now claim as "quality time."

The care and nurturing of children has challenged all generations. When mothers work, however, who is to provide that care and nurturing?

During World War II, women worked in the country's factories in large numbers so that essential production could continue while men were at war. These women still had to fulfill their roles as homemakers, leaving after eight hours on an assembly line to shop, cook, clean, and care for their families. Stores were not open after work— twenty-four-hour Safeways are a relatively new option. Most women found it impossible to maintain both a wartime factory job and their home responsibilities. Over a four-year period, Boeing employed 250,000 women to maintain a labor force of 39,000. (William H. Chafe, *The American Woman*, Oxford University Press, 1972, p. 159.) Absenteeism and the high turnover of women laborers posed critical problems for the war effort.

The federal government was asked to create community child-care centers but balked at interfering in family relationships. Meanwhile, child-neglect cases mounted, and women were sometimes left with no alternative other than to leave their children locked in a car at the war-plant parking lot. In 1943, the Roosevelt administration determined that money set aside for wartime facilities could be used to build and operate day-care centers. Local governments were required to put up 50 percent of the cost. (*Id.*, p. 166.)

Communities that sought to establish child-care centers were met with a bureaucratic maze; seven government agencies were involved in the program. At the height of these efforts, only 100,000 children (less than 10 percent of those who needed it) were helped by federally supported facilities. (*Id.*, p. 170.)

Individual companies that needed women workers sometimes contributed to the effort. Kaiser staffed and financed a twenty-four-hour-a-day community school for children from eighteen months to six years in Portland, Oregon. Some communities found that they could use existing buildings and resources. Faculty wives and student teachers helped stretch the capacity of Vancouver, Washington's school system to include an after-school program for children and to accommodate a tripling of school enrollment in the first two years of the war. (*Id.*, pp. 162–163.)

After World War II, women returned to their homes (many unwillingly forced to relinquish their positions to returning soldiers) and created the image of family life that I grew up with. *Ozzie and Harriet, Father Knows Best*, and *The Donna Reed Show* instructed families in the 1950s on the parameters of the American dream. Single-family homes in suburbia became the rage, and we increasingly separated working dads from responsibilities for family life. Postwar America returned with gusto to the image of mother behind an apron, baking cookies and worrying about her washing detergent.

Women have now rejected this limited vision of their roles. Particularly during the 1970s, they discovered a political accident that assisted them in the workplace. When Congress considered the Civil Rights Act of 1964, some Southerners tried to derail the effort by tacking on gender as a prohibited basis for employment decisions. (110 Cong. Rec. 2577–2584, 2718, 2720–2721 [1964].) No one took the preposterous idea particularly seriously: In 1970, six years later, I was frankly advised by my employer that he was paying me less than a man with a less responsible position because the fellow was, after all, male. (I quit.)

However, the failed effort to stop the civil rights bill turned into a powerful weapon to open doors to women in the workplace. Gender discrimination lawsuits have forced a rethinking of job bias throughout America, starting with a ban on classified ads that list jobs as "Men Only." Women have shown up in unusual positions: After a decade-long court battle, the Pacific Maritime Association and the Longshoreman's Union agreed to fill 35 percent of part-time dockworker jobs and 17.5 percent of full-time jobs with women. Three hundred fifty part-time jobs were immediately opened up for women by the settlement of the suit: Over 6,000 women applied. ("More Than 6,000 Women Seek Dockworker Jobs," *Los Angeles Times*, June 19, 1990.) When I served as Chairman of the Federal Mine Safety and Health Review Commission, my role in the mining business was so unusual that it became the subject of a short video. Thousands of women are performing similar nontraditional jobs.

Women face impediments in the labor force at all levels of employment, from the loading dock to the executive suite. The U.S. Department of Labor (DOL) has recently announced a major investigation into a phenomenon labeled the "glass ceiling," a term that refers to invisible barriers that prevent women and minorities from obtaining executive-level positions. ("OFCCP to Study Role of Minorities, Women at Top of Corporate Ladder," *Daily Labor Report*, September 12, 1990.) The statistics may be unnerving to those who believe that women have already won the feminist battles of the 1970s.

Fortune magazine examined lists of the highest-paid officers and directors of the 799 public companies on its list of the 1,000 largest American industrial and service companies. Of the 4,012 names it found, only 19 were those of women. A similar study in 1978—a dozen years ago—revealed 10 women in the highest ranks of corporate America.

The obvious answer is that women are in the pipeline, readying themselves for promotions that will vault them into corner offices. But *Fortune* found that of 9,292 division heads and assistant vice presidents in 255 major corporations, only 5 percent are women. ("Why Women Still Don't Hit the Top," *Fortune*, July 30, 1990.)

Fortune concluded that the barrier to promotions is not that women are dividing time and attention between their jobs and their families but rather that a new form of sex discrimination is to blame. The blatant sexism of the past may be gone, when all women, no matter what their level or experience, were asked to pour coffee. But more subtle sexism continues to persist.

The new sexism may take various forms. Subtle stereotyping and assumptions about women continue, and many men will deny that these long-held beliefs are even sexist. Many men view a short, soft-spoken woman with alarm and worry that she does not have the "presence" to be in charge, so they do not offer her the opportunity. They fail to see any contradiction when, at the same time, they concede that such an unacceptable woman is a "walking encyclopedia" in her field and knows more substantively than male counterparts and that a tall, soft-spoken man would be quite acceptable. Women are often viewed as less aggressive and less competitive (which are watchwords for "not as good as a man") or as brash, pushy, and bitchy. Women themselves share these perceptions with the male world: Marion Howington, retired senior vice president at J. Walter Thompson, has said that success requires a woman to "think like a man" and that "there's not a woman anywhere who made it in business who is not tough, self-centered and enormously aggressive." ("Why Can't a Woman Manager Be More Like . . . A Woman?" *Time*, Special Issue, Fall 1990, p. 53.) While I personally reject Ms. Howington's approach, I must admit to reacting with some squeamishness to the statement of Sandra Kurtzig, founder and president of ASK Computer Systems, that she has "a style of walking around and stroking people. ... I try to compliment them in front of their peers and *go up and hug them.*" (*Ibid.* Emphasis added.) It seems on balance that a woman who develops a different, more nurturing management style is often stepped over and viewed as weak, even by other women.

Men are often still uncomfortable accepting women as peers; women do not fit the old-boy Brooks Brothers corporate image. Louise LaMothe (a partner at Irell & Manella and vice-chair of the 60,000-member American Bar Association Litigation Section) has written of the problems she faces as an extraordinarily successful woman in a traditionally male part of the profession. (The first women lawyers were carefully directed to "family" matters like divorce and wills and far away from juries and courtrooms.) As a partner, Ms. LaMothe's status in the firm is linked not only to the quality of her work but also to the number of clients she attracts. LaMothe says, "It's clear to me ... that if women are not placed on a more equal footing in terms of bringing in business, they are never going to be able to make the kind of progress in private law firms that they need to establish themselves as serious contenders." LaMothe comments on how few women have sent her business. "I have been, and probably will continue to be throughout my legal career, dependent on men to send me business. ... I think we all have to recognize the way business is passed around is virtually through an old-boy, and I do mean old-boy, network. Until that begins to change, we're not going to see any real change in terms of the power that women wield in the profession," she concludes. ("Profile,"

The Los Angeles Daily Journal, August 7, 1990.)

The Labor Department is investigating the upper echelons of companies that do business with the federal government to determine why women and minorities appear to be stopped short of upper-level management positions. One practice under scrutiny is a selection process that depends on informal word-of-mouth through established contacts and networks. Such a system may have the effect, if not the intent, of excluding qualified women and minorities who do not play golf or who are not otherwise "plugged in" to the grapevine.

The DOL investigations find some support in the recent Supreme Court decision in *Price Waterhouse v. Hopkins.* (490 U.S. 228, 109 S. Ct. 1775 [1989].) Ann Hopkins alleged that Price Waterhouse denied her a promotion to partnership because of sex discrimination. Price Waterhouse had 876 partners at the time, of whom 27 were women. Hopkins had an impressive record of admirable work and had played a major role in securing contracts worth over $40 million for the firm. She was rejected for partnership based on negative personal comments in her review. Her chief supporter, for one, had advised her that to be successful, she had to "walk more femininely, talk more femininely, wear makeup, have [her] hair styled, and wear jewelry." The Supreme Court found the use of such criteria to evidence sex discrimination in the promotion process. A federal judge has since ordered Price Waterhouse to pay Hopkins $370,000 in back pay and to make her a partner.

Expectations of how workers should look and act create a hazardous area for men and women alike. Youthful-looking women especially face the obstacle of credibility:

When one is repeatedly greeted by the exclamation, "But you're so young," it requires a constant effort to be deemed competent. When I was the head of a government agency, I once force-transferred an older woman who was supposed to be my aide because she continuously introduced me by saying, "This is my boss. Can you believe she's so young?" As noted by Ms. LaMothe, when a woman lawyer looks young, clients "just don't believe you could be good. So you have to prove that to each new client and that's exhausting after a while." ("Profile," *Los Angeles Daily Journal*, August 7, 1990.)

Exhaustion is an experience common to women who make it to the top of their fields, especially if they also have family responsibilities. But most women do not quit executive positions to care for children. In a survey called "Don't Blame the Baby," Wick and Co., a consulting firm, found that only 7 percent of those surveyed left their positions to stay home. Women, like men, change jobs to advance their careers. In a study of women making $40,000 to $100,000 annually, 73 percent of the women who left their jobs went to work for other companies and 13 percent left to start their own businesses. Women owned more than twice as many companies in 1987 as they did ten years earlier. ("Kids Aren't the Only Reason Women Leave Their Jobs," *Chicago Tribune*, July 23, 1990.)

The perception that women leave high-paying jobs to have children, never to return to their careers, was addressed in a *Harvard Business Review* article by Felice Schwartz, president and founder of Catalyst, a not-for-profit research and advisory organization in New York City that works with corporations to foster careers and leadership development of women. Schwartz is now notorious for a concept others have dubbed the "Mommy Track." Her article discusses the hard questions that arise when women become executive level employees. Because of maternity leave, women are perceived as more expensive to employ than men. Schwartz argues that stereotyped views exaggerate the potential extra costs to the detriment of all women, regardless of their family circumstances.

Schwartz identifies two categories of gender differences that may be relevant to business: "those related to maternity and those related to the differing traditions of the sexes." She notes that, in a developed society, only childbearing is uniquely gender related. It is, Schwartz argues, the differences between the socialization of men and that of women that can create unnecessary conflict in the workplace.

Since business needs women employees, and women need and want to work, Schwartz proposes that women should be viewed as either "career-primary" or "career-and-family." It is this distinction that has made Schwartz's proposal so controversial, for her detractors accuse her of advocating a dead-end "Mommy Track" for those women who want to combine career and family.

Schwartz bases her analysis, in part, on the fact that 90 percent of executives who are male have children by the age of 40, while only 35 percent of executive females have children by that time. Her conclusion is that the other 65 percent of executive women should have all artificial barriers removed from their path to success. According to Schwartz, the remaining 35 percent of women **executives**, who want to combine career and family, should be content with middle-management positions where ostensibly they can enjoy continued challenges and more flexible schedules. ("Management Women and the Real Facts of Life," *Harvard Business Review*, January–February 1989.)

The failure to challenge the bases for the disparity between male and female executives with children has caused Schwartz's article to come under attack from those who argue that women with children remain just as qualified, just as motivated, and just as deserving of progress up the corporate ladder as any male.

The debate is over whether, in this society, women can "have it all," whether a woman can combine family and a successful career. Many women would still agree with suffragist Crystal Eastman, who wrote in 1918, "Women who are creative, or who have administrative gifts, or business ability, and who are ambitious to achieve and fulfill themselves in these lives, if they also have the normal desire to be mothers, must make up their minds to be a sort of supermen [sic!] I think. They must develop greater powers of concentration, a stronger will to 'keep at it,' a more determined ambition than men of equal gifts, in order to make up for the time and energy and thought and devotion that childbearing and rearing, even in the most 'advanced' families, seem inexorably to demand of the mother." (Eastman, "The Birth Control Review," January 1918, collected in *On Women and Revolution*, ed. by Blanche Wiesen Cook, Oxford University Press, 1978, p. 47). Charlotte Whitton, the former mayor of Ottawa, echoes the same thought today in a quip that makes women laugh and wince. Says Whitton, "[W]hatever women do, they must do twice as well as men to be thought half as good. Luckily, this is not difficult." ("The Dreams of Youth," *Time*, Special Issue, Fall 1990, p. 12.)

Schwartz's categorizing of women into career-primary and career-and-family attracted notoriety because it seemed to say that women could not have it all. They could have a lot perhaps—a family and a topped-out career or no family and a career without bounds—but a combination of family and full career success was impossible. More apt than Schwartz, William James identified the real stress point, although in another context: "The actually possible in this world is vastly narrower than all that is demanded; and there is always a pinch between the ideal and the actual which can only be got through by leaving part of the ideal behind." (William James, "The Moral Philosopher and the Moral Life (1891)," *The Will to Believe and Other Essays in Popular Philosophy*, Harvard University Press, 1979, p. 153).

As women have moved from the family orientation of the 1950s through the career orientation of the 1970s, we have come to the time when today's young women talk of career, children, and family in a "balance" that has so far eluded the rest of us. Schwartz, I think, is wrong to suggest that it is not possible to have both family and successful career, but having both remains difficult for all participants, who inevitably lose some of the ideal.

We do not have a crisis like World War II forcing us to create support mechanisms for working mothers. However, these women, who are a vital part of the American labor force, are finding that they cannot do it all. The last decade has seen families, communities, business, and governments struggle with the issues of working women and how society will care for its children.

Child care is perhaps the most visible way that society—from government to business—confronts the rising number of women in the labor force. Increasingly, companies are finding that on-site day care is a cost-effective fringe benefit. Absenteeism decreases and productivity increases when workers are able to work without worrying about the safety of their children.

Working Mother magazine compiled a list of the seventy-five companies it considers the "best" for working mothers. ("The 75 Best Companies for Working Mothers," *Working Mother*, October 1990.) All offer some form of child-care assistance, from subsidies to on-site day care. Working mothers find that flexible schedules and shared jobs can ease the burdens. IBM now offers a three-year maternity leave with full benefits if an employee is available for part-time work after the first year. Large companies with the capital to initiate such programs often find that the cost of retaining qualified and trained employees is less than that of dealing with turnover; such programs may also be effective recruitment tools to attract talented women.

The tough issue is the role of the government in addressing this shared problem of American society. If government assumes responsibility for assuring adequate child care—whether through Head Start program guarantees, tax breaks, establishment of day-care centers, or subsidies for child care—who will teach moral values to our children? Is child care merely a question of logistics—food, shelter, and an occasional hug—or does it require more? The "balance" sought by women in their twenties cannot be achieved by merely assuring adequate supervision of their children while the mothers work, although that is a basic need. My assumption sixteen years ago that the logistics of obtaining a baby-sitter were all that stood between me and my career is regularly proven wrong, even as my son matures to the point where he baby-sits for others.

One impact on family life that is apparent from the development of large numbers of working women is that women bear children later in life than they used to and in smaller numbers. While my mother had nine children and cheered me through law school and into a career, I have had only one, born just before I turned thirty, back at a time when that age was considered the important time line for childbearing. Today, a mere eyeblink later, a woman's biological clock is thought to keep ticking at least into her early forties, and more and more career women are waiting later and later to begin their families. Those women over forty whom Schwartz thought had committed themselves to their careers have now begun to bear their own children.

At the other end of the spectrum, we have growing numbers of very young single girls giving birth. Children having children complicate family life and the transmission of values from generation to generation in much more fundamental ways than does the advent of late childbearing.

We really face one issue on two different planes. On one level, we must as a society address the pure logistics of caring for the next generations. Younger women lawyers with whom I work see this issue as very much one for government action and intervention: They are willing to state categorically that there is a role for government in the formation of child-care policies. They liken access to government-sponsored child care to access to government-sponsored mass transportation. Both, they argue, are necessary if America's mothers are to be able to work and support their families.

On a deeper, more difficult level, the problem lies in the topic of these lectures: how to continue traditions and values from generation to generation when parents and children spend so little time together. Exhausted parents have little flexibility to support their children's personalities once the children's basic needs are met. Our present difficulties with attending to our children lie not so much with the fact that their mothers work outside the home as with the generally frantic pace of life in twentieth-century America. Whatever any of us does with our days, we are all too rushed and haggard by day's end. Who, male or female, has time to write the loving letters crafted by Civil War soldiers that we recently found so moving on the PBS specials about that war?

The impact for family life brought about by increasing numbers of women in the workplace boils down to one issue: the availability of time. Obviously, hours spent at a desk or a lathe or teaching a class are not hours that can be spent with a mother's own children. This loss of family time affects both men and women in the pace of today's world but shows up most starkly in comparing the roles of women in the 1950s and in the 1990s. Our mental picture of a "family" has mother at home with the children while father is out earning the head-of-household income. Now that both mother and father are working, or mother is left alone to cope with job and children, we fear that the "family" is a lost element of life. And, in fact, for many children growing up in America today, the 1950s image of family is unexperienced and unimaginable.

When time together is lessened, so are opportunities for sharing and conveying the traditions that distinguish one family or culture from another. When my son was young and his parents had more time, we all made batches of fancy Christmas cookies from Grandma's cookbook. We have not made Christmas cookies in years. My son does not remember the early years and does not know the joys of snickerdoodles. Out of such simple and relatively unimportant changes in life-style comes a loss of connectedness to his own past and family. Traditions must be established over time; they cannot be experienced only once or twice and retain their meaning. It is somewhat frightening how quickly they can be lost for good.

How much time does a working mother have to spend nurturing her children in the traditions that distinguish the family? The Family Research Council in Washington, D.C., estimates that the "total contact time" between parents and children has dropped to 40 percent in the last twenty-five years. Time is boiled down to its bare essentials during the workweek: a generally hurried and frequently ill-tempered getting children up and out in the morning and a race at night to collect the children, prepare supper, oversee homework, and get everyone to bed. A full-time working mother will see her young children no more than two to three hours a day. Working mothers with infants might not see their babies awake for days on end if work emergencies cause the mothers to stay late or to go to work early.

Every working mother makes her own adjustments and trade-offs as she struggles to be mother and laborer. Instead of locking their children in the car in the plant parking lot, mothers give housekeys to their children so they can let themselves in at the end of the school day. One four-year-old reported that he did not need to worry if he lost his key; he was small enough to crawl in through the dog's flap. Enormous numbers of latchkey children are essentially raising themselves.

Why is this happening? Families find themselves dealing with economic pressures from two sides: Their income is affected by lower wages and higher taxes, and their expenses for homes, insurance, and education have soared. Mothers have entered the work force in dramatically large numbers in an effort to stabilize family income, but many working women do not have the skills to obtain high-paying jobs. Raised during the 1950s with the expectation of becoming homemakers, many working women are prepared only for jobs, not careers. Regardless of their earning power, women who work have less time to spend with their families.

One cost of this process has been the creation of a tremendous sense of guilt among parents about the consequences for their children. We do not know, as a society, what those consequences may be, but, as parents, we all worry constantly. Since time together is so precious, few parents want to squander it on discipline. Children of all ages quickly learn that they can get away with conduct that is unacceptable just because their parents do not want the entire parental role defined by scolding and punishment. To keep our children behaving, we tend to give them distractions—television, Nintendo, pop music—so that we have a few moments of peace. What values do they learn from such teachers?

Religious beliefs, commonly shared across whole communities, used to provide a moral base for all. One unfortunate consequence of women's burgeoning sense of independent worth is a rejection of some elements of organized religion. The successful woman with a job that challenges her every day is not likely to agree that she is a mere handmaiden to her husband or that, as the traditional marriage ceremony suggests, she must be submissive and obedient. Churches that do not welcome women as full participants in all aspects of church life increasingly discover that women are not in attendance. There is a great tension between the workplace, where a woman must assert her worth regularly to be heard and listened to, and a church service that preaches that she must be silent and accepting of male domination. As a result, whole families are growing up without the teachings of any church at all. Values and traditions that once bound us together are lost to our children. Of course, problems with our children are much larger than the issue of working mothers. Early this fall *Time* reported that

> "every eight seconds of the school day, a child drops out. Every 26 seconds, a child runs away from home. Every 47 seconds a child is abused or neglected. Every 67 seconds a teenager has a baby. Every seven minutes a child is arrested for a drug offense. Every 36 minutes a child is killed or injured by a gun. Every day 135,000 children bring their guns to school." ("Shameful Bequests to the Next Generation," *Time*, October 8, 1990.)

America must address these problems if a truly free

society, which requires educated and committed peoples, is to remain. One premise we must accept is that increasing numbers of women do and will work outside their homes. I suggest that it is time to jettison *Father Knows Best*. Let's deal with the realities of the future and not pine for the brief interlude after World War II when a fast-growing economy and a huge influx of male workers momentarily freed women to define themselves as homemakers and not breadwinners. Life is just as real now as it was in the 1890s or 1790s, when most women made essential contributions to their family incomes. Let's move on from that reality.

Reality suggests that the future American work force will contain greater numbers of diverse people with diverse talents and needs. As the "baby bust" generation matures, the work force will grow much more slowly than in the past. Two-thirds of that increase is expected to be women starting or returning to work. Can these needed workers combine family and career?

In one area, that question must be answered by the Supreme Court. A recently argued case involves a battery manufacturer that has barred fertile women from working in positions where their unborn children might be exposed to dangerous levels of lead. The company argues that it cannot totally remove the lead from the environment and still make batteries. Exposures are controlled to avoid harm to adults, but very small amounts of lead can harm a fetus. In order to avoid such harm, the company requires women to prove they cannot bear children or to accept less favorable positions. The question before the Supreme Court is whether such a fetal-protection policy impermissibly discriminates against women. The courts have split on the issue, with the Seventh Circuit upholding the company's policy and the California Court of Appeals finding "blatant" discrimination and commenting, "A woman is not required to be a Victorian broodmare." (*United Auto Workers v. Johnson Controls, Inc.*, 886 F.2d 871 [7th Cir. 1988], *cert. granted*, 110 S. Ct. 1522 [1990]; *Johnson Controls, Inc. v. California Fair Employment & Housing Comm'n*, 267 Cal. Rptr. 158, 218 Cal. App. 3d 517 [Cal. Ct. App. 1990].)

Women argue that barring them from well-paying jobs merely because they have the capability of becoming pregnant is rank discrimination. Companies, fearing liability for deformed infants, think they have no options. It is doubtful that a woman could effectively sign a waiver excusing an employer from all liability for harm to her unborn child: Mothers of children born with a drug addiction because of drugs taken during pregnancy are finding themselves at the receiving end of criminal charges for harming their children. Cases involving prenatal drug delivery have been initiated in nine states so far, and eight states are considering legislation that would criminalize drug or alcohol abuse that harmed an unborn child. ("Do the Unborn Have Rights?" *Time*, Special Issue, Fall 1990.) Battery manufacturers face an unenviable Catch-22: Barring fertile women from exposure to substances that are known to harm a fetus leads to sex discrimination lawsuits, while admitting women to such jobs could lead to even more awful results and liability for harm to the unborn.

The Supreme Court case, *United Auto Workers v. Johnson Controls, Inc.*, demonstrates one thing: Women cannot, in fact, safely have it all.

Nonetheless, the increase of women in the work force will only continue. As a society, we are wrestling with the effects of that change both in the workplace and at home. Clinging to a past vision, we continue to structure society around the notion that women are available to raise children, care for elderly parents, and tend houses. They are not. We need to restructure our thoughts, expectations, and actions.

Families will be smaller as women continue to work. The woman who has three or more children finds it economically and physically impossible to maintain any career track. The *Washington Post* recently chronicled the story of a divorced mother of three children. Without federal child-care subsidies, her annual child-care cost for her younger two children was over $7,000, which did not leave enough for the $40 needed for after-school care for her oldest child, an eight-year-old. This girl was forced to stay by herself at home every day after school. The woman took another job, with fewer demands, fewer chances for promotion, and less money, so that she would be eligible for federal subsidies. With the subsidy, her annual child-care cost for all three children dropped to $360. ("Mother Takes Pay Cut to Get Day Care," *The Washington Post*, June 25, 1990.) In effect, she traded her own future for her children's sake.

Money is not the only issue. My firm recently lost a highly successful woman partner, who left to teach because she could not maintain a demanding trial practice and give sufficient time and attention to her family, which includes a newborn third child. Sheer physical and emotional exhaustion overcame her.

Both mothers continue to work, despite the demands of

their families. Their experiences demonstrate the truism reflected in my own life: Large families and successful careers are particularly hard to mix.

Jobs will be restructured in the future. As a "veteran" of the first wave of working mothers into the workplace, I shake my head at the dreams of younger women that they will handle without stress the jobs of motherhood and career. But those with determination will remake this society. Business already needs intelligent workers of any gender or color; those needs will only be magnified in future years. Shared jobs will cease to be a rarity. Work at home will cease to be seen as a cop-out. Emergency on-site child care, for snow days and those occasions when sitters are ill, will multiply. Part-time positions will be increasingly substantive and less often only mind numbing. Time away from work for school affairs and Little League games will be more accepted as a cost of doing business. Pressure will continue on governments at all levels to contribute positively to resolving issues of child care.

Will this nirvana be reached quickly or easily? Of course not. For society to change takes years of grueling effort, of dealing with the consequences of failure to change, before a consensus can develop that will alter our fundamental perceptions of a woman's place. We will change only because the situation will not allow us to retain the status quo. As they say, necessity is the mother of invention, and we need that mothering to start now.

THE SEXUAL DIVISION OF LABOR, THE DECLINE OF CIVIC CULTURE, AND THE RISE OF THE SUBURBS

by

Christopher Lasch

Christopher Lasch

Christopher Lasch is Don Alonzo Washington Professor of History and Chairman of the Department of History at the University of Rochester. Before coming to the University of Rochester in 1970, Professor Lasch taught at Williams College, Roosevelt University, the University of Iowa, and Northwestern University.

Professor Lasch received his B.A. degree from Harvard College and his M.A. and Ph.D. degrees from Columbia University. He has received honorary degrees from Bard College and Hobart and William Smith College.

His books include The American Liberals and the Russian Revolution *(1962),* The New Radicalism in America, 1889–1963: The Intellectual as a Social Type *(1965),* The Agony of the American Left *(1969),* Haven in a Heartless World: The Family Besieged *(1977),* The Culture of Narcissism *(1979), and* The Minimal Self: Psychic Survival in Troubled Times *(1984). His works have been translated into thirteen languages. A new book,* The True and Only Heaven: Progress and Its Critics, *appeared in the fall of 1990.*

Professor Lasch was a member of the editorial board of democracy, *a political quarterly, and is a consulting editor of* Tikkun. *He was the Freud Memorial Lecturer at University College London in 1989 and was at the Center for Advanced Study in the Behavioral Sciences in 1988–89. He was awarded the Bowdoin Prize at Harvard in 1954 and declined the American Book Award in 1980.*

THE SEXUAL DIVISION OF LABOR, THE DECLINE OF CIVIC CULTURE, AND THE RISE OF THE SUBURBS

by

Christopher Lasch

The history of women, as the media have taught us to understand it, falls into two epochs, divided by the sexual revolution of the sixties. It was only in the sixties, according to the media's foreshortened view of things, that women began their painful climb out of the sexual dark ages. They entered the work force, gained control over their own bodies, and challenged male supremacy in all its forms—political, economic, ideological. Until then, women labored under age-old disabilities. Since the sixties, they have "come a long way," and although the revolution against patriarchy still has a long way to go before women gain full equality, it is irresistible. There can be no going back to the old days, to the "traditional" arrangements that kept women at home and left men in control of the great world outside.

It is this undifferentiated image of the old days that I want to call into question—the impression that women's lives used to be taken up entirely by the demands of housework and motherhood. In reality, full-time motherhood—the rejection of which touched off the latest wave of feminist agitation in the sixties—was something new and historically unprecedented. It was largely a product of the rapid growth of suburbs after World War II, and the feminist revival initiated by Betty Friedan's *The*

Feminine Mystique originated as a direct response, often a very self-conscious response, not to the age-old oppression of women, but to the suburbanization of the American soul. Only later did the feminist movement come to understand the condition it sought to change—the division of labor that confined women to the home—as a "patriarchal" system that could be found, with minor variations, in all times and places. In the popular mind, the division of labor that prevailed in postwar suburbia thus came to be identified—with a corresponding loss of intellectual clarity—with the division of sexual labor in general.

All societies distinguish between women's work and men's work. Such distinctions are often invidious, serving to keep women in a subordinate status. It is only recently, however, that "woman's place" has been defined in such a way as to exclude her from participation in the common life beyond the household. The modern home, which presupposes a radical separation of domestic life from the world of work, was an invention of the nineteenth century. The decline of household production and the rise of wage labor made it possible—made it necessary—to conceive of the family as a private retreat from a public world increasingly dominated by the impersonal mechanisms of the market. The image of the family as a haven in a heartless world helped Americans to manage the ambivalent emotions evoked by the new industrial order. On the one hand, they wanted the comforts and conveniences furnished by industrial progress; on the other hand, the agency of progress—the capitalist market—appeared to foster a type of acquisitive individualism that left no room for the finer things in life: loving-kindness, spontaneous affection, what John Stuart Mill called the "culture of feelings." By assigning custody of "feelings" to the family, people tried to reassure themselves that values rooted in "ascription," as the sociologists say—recognition of persons that does not have to be earned but is merely bestowed—would continue to have a place even in societies governed by the principle of competitive achievement.

The nineteenth-century cult of domesticity, as historians have come to call it, revolved around a new glorification of motherhood. But the rhetoric of motherhood and domesticity cannot be taken as an accurate or complete description of women's lives in the nineteenth and early twentieth centuries. Housework and child care by no means exhausted women's energies. On the contrary, both housewives and single women threw themselves into a variety of activities that took them out of the home. They organized benevolent societies, female reform societies, and foreign missions. They put together a vast network of temperance societies. They took up charities and philanthropies of all kinds. Many of them enlisted in the antislavery crusade, the peace movement, prison reform, and of course the movement for women's rights. Historians have known for a long time that women played a central part in all the reform movements that swept over the country in the nineteenth century, not to mention the evangelical revivals that furnished much of the moral inspiration behind those movements; but they have somehow failed to connect these activities with the subject of women's work. For historians as for everybody else, work is understood as something dignified by a salary or a wage. Uncompensated activity, though it enters the historical record under the heading of "reform," is seldom recognized as a form of productive work, even when it brought women into the public world in great numbers. The impression that nineteenth-century women were confined to the domestic "sphere" thus remains undisturbed by the record of their active participation in the "world's work," as they themselves liked to refer to it.

Women's voluntary participation in the public world probably reached its high point in the years between 1890 and 1920, the so-called progressive era, which also coincided with the final stages of the campaign for woman suffrage. "Between 1890 and 1920," wrote the historian Mary Ryan, "women built a rationalized organizational network that was nearly as sophisticated in its own way as the corporate business world." The General Federation of Women's Clubs, organized in 1890, is estimated to have included two million members by 1910. Another two million took part in the movement for woman suffrage. In 1920, half a million women belonged to the Young Women's Christian Association, and almost a million to the Women's Christian Temperance Union. The rapid growth of the National Council of Jewish Women, founded in 1893, indicates that the volunteering impulse was not confined to white Anglo-Saxon Protestants. The establishment of the National Association of Colored Women, in 1895, preceded the founding of the National Association for the Advancement of Colored People by fifteen years. The National Consumers League, the Women's Trade Union League, the Women's International League for Peace and Freedom, and innumerable other organizations, many of them now forgotten, enlisted the efforts of volunteers in a wide range of good causes. The progressive era was the age of "social housekeeping," when women aspired "to make the whole world homelike," in the words of Florence Willard of the WCTU. Women demanded the vote on the grounds that maternal "influence" should not be confined to the home. But they did not wait for the vote to legitimize their reforming efforts; nor were they handicapped by the lack of it. Indeed there is reason to think that women were more active citizens before getting the vote than afterwards, in part because they had so much stake in proving that they could act responsibly in the public realm. They took part in, and often initiated, movements to abolish child labor, to establish juvenile courts, to build slum housing, to require factory inspection, to strengthen the food and drug laws, and to abolish or regulate prostitution. "Scarcely without exception," according to Judge Ben Lindsey, one of the prominent reformers of the time, "it has been the members of the women's clubs . . . who have secured the passage of all the advanced legislation . . . for the protection of the home and the child."

Social reform was the most visible but by no means the exclusive or even the most important contribution made by women to public life. Their work as volunteers sustained a vast array of public services—libraries, hospitals, nursery schools, social settlements, parks, playgrounds, concert halls, museums. The progressive era was the heyday of the "city beautiful," when American cities built public facilities and amenities designed to bring culture to the masses and to encourage widespread participation in civic life. The reformer Frederic C. Howe spoke for his entire generation when he referred to the city as the "hope of democracy." Today it is fashionable to deprecate the civic architecture of those years as a

monument to imperial grandeur and to sneer at "uplift"
as an imposition of middle-class values on the immigrant
poor. But uplift was not yet identified with "Americani-
zation," and the public buildings that served to advertise
America's commercial and military power also served
to give ordinary people access to the nation's culture.
Mary Antin, in her 1912 memoir of a girlhood spent in
Russia and in the Jewish ghetto of South Boston, cap-
tured something of the promise of this urban awakening
when she described the Boston Public Library as the
"chamber of [her] dreams." With the carved inscription
over its doors, "Built by the People—Free to All," the library brought home to her the "wonder of my life." "That
I who was born in the prison of the Pale . . . [and] brought
up to my teens almost without a book should be set down
in the midst of all the books that ever were written was
a miracle as great as any on record." No doubt Antin's
account of immigrant life omitted some of its darker aspects, but it showed how much a great American city
could offer to those who were able and willing to seize it.

These impressive resources, the foundations of which
were laid down for the most part in the great age of
American urbanism, were largely sustained, I suspect,
by the unpaid labor of women, who raised the money,
performed the daily drudgery, and furnished much of
the moral vision behind the civic renewal of the early
twentieth century. I am in no position to prove the point
at this stage in my research, but it does not seem fanciful
to suggest that it was women, toiling almost invariably
behind the scenes and without monetary reward, who
made the city liveable, prevented it from becoming a
place devoted to business alone, and kept alive the vision

of a civic culture open to all. Henry James observed, in *The American Scene* (1907), that the "interests of civilization," of "social property" and "social office," were carried on by women, while American men devoted themselves single-mindedly to business—that is, to private affairs, as they would have been described in Europe. Women, James wrote, had established "peerless possession" of all forms of public life in the true sense, of art, learning, and sociability; and although this arrangement—"the sentence written largest in the American sky"—struck him as deeply regrettable, since it meant that the "whole plane of the amenities" remained "residual" in a business civilization, it nevertheless provided Americans with as much civic culture as they had managed to achieve.

The American Scene, incidentally, contains a description of the Boston Public Library that should be set beside Mary Antin's. Comparing the new building in Copley Square to European libraries, James was struck by its accessibility, its rejection of any suggestion of the mystery or sacred space—*"penetralia"*—normally associated with a place of learning. A "library without *penetralia*" struck James as slightly incongruous, a "temple without altars." "The British Museum, the Louvre, the Bibliotheque Nationale, the Treasures of South Kensington, are assuredly ... at the disposal of the people; but it is to be observed, I think, that the people walk there more or less under the shadow of the right waited for and conceded." The more democratic conception of culture embodied in the Boston Public Library, experienced by James as a "reservation" to his pleasure in the new building, was exactly what commended the place to a young woman from the slums.

James's misgivings about the democratization of culture may strike us as misplaced, but his account of the division of sexual labor provides a useful corrective to conventional accounts, which assume that unless women work in professional careers they must be confined to the home and which therefore miss women's contribution to an intermediate realm of civic culture that belongs neither to the family nor to the market. *The American Scene* is also useful, for our present purposes, because it enables us to see that the revulsion against the so-called genteel tradition, so clearly foreshadowed in James's book, was among other things a revulsion against the influence of women as custodians of American culture. In 1926, twenty years after the publication of *The American Scene*, Thomas Beer opened his influential little book, *The Mauve Decade* with a savage attack on the "Titaness"—the American woman as arbiter of public taste and morals. By the 1890s, Beer wrote, "the Middle Western woman had quietly become a fixture on the American social chart, a shadowy Titaness, a terror to editors, the hope of missionary societies and the prey of lecturers." Animated by an "instinctive envy of all that was free, cool, or unhaltered," she had lost sight of whatever was "honourable in the Bostonian tradition," retaining only its "confusion of morals with manners." Together with "her more restrained sisters of the East and West," she tyrannized over the arts and made politicians tremble with her many-sided campaign for "social purity." No lapse of taste or decorum was too small to escape her attention, according to Beer. "She was an emblem, a grotesque shape in hot black silk, screaming threats at naked children in a clear river, with her companionable ministers and reformers at heel." She attended "congress after congress for the correction of mankind." Her censorship of literature bespoke a "resolute violence of the cheapest kind, without breeding, without taste." No doubt she did not invent "cheap cruelty and low social pressures," but she "erected these basenesses into virtues by some defensive sense of rectitude, and a generation of sons was reared in the shadow of the Titaness, aware of her power, protected by nothing from her shrill admonitions."

It took more than satire, whether in the form of Beer's venom or the gentler ridicule of Helen Hokinson, to drive women out of the public forum, but satire must have played some part in their postwar retreat from civic causes and campaigns. In the twenties, club women, do-gooders, "upbuilders," and cultural missionaries became symbols of Victorian repression or, at best, figures of fun. The flapper, not the feminist, now served as the prototype of the emancipated woman; the battle of the sexes shifted from the lecture circuit to the bedroom; and the assertion of women's equal right to sexual pleasure absorbed energies formerly devoted to social reform and civic improvement. The professionalization of these activities further contributed to the decline of voluntary public service. Settlement houses were taken over by professional social workers, charities by professional administrators. A sociological investigation carried out many years later, *Life Styles of Educated Women*, by Eli Ginzberg and his associates, reported that "volunteer organizations have come more and more under the control and direction of full-time professional staff.

While there is still a place for the volunteer either as a board member or as a worker, the scope for her participation in many organizations has been substantially reduced." The same consideration led Morton Hunt, in his 1962 study of American women, *Her Infinite Variety*, to conclude that although "perhaps ten to fifteen million women do volunteer work for various community agencies," these impressive numbers "mean less than they seem to." Voluntary service had never recovered the prestige it enjoyed in the nineteenth and early twentieth centuries. Women now had to choose between a home and a career, and the choice had become so familiar that people soon forgot that there had ever been any other.

Volunteer work commended itself to women, in the age of its efflorescence, in part because it was easily combined with domestic responsibilities, unlike the inflexible schedules imposed by paid work. Those responsibilities, moreover, were themselves less burdensome than they subsequently became, since most women were able to count on help from domestic servants, in-laws and relatives, and their own children. The "benevolent empire" of nineteenth-century women, including the feminist movement itself, "was underwritten by the household labors of domestic servants," as Faye Dudden noted in her study of household service, *Serving Women*. In the twentieth century, however, live-in domestic servants gradually disappeared from American households, except from those of the very rich, and even part-time servants grew harder and harder to find. Immigration restriction, compulsory education, and the availability of less demeaning jobs in factories and offices choked off the supply of domestics, while new standards of domestic privacy (together with a drastic shrinkage in the size of middle-class houses) made the employment of live-in servants seem undesirable in any case. But the decline of domestic service was not the only development that altered the structure of the American household. In the past, the household economy always rested, in part, on the exchange of unpaid services among relatives, friends, and neighbors, as Mary Howell reminded us some years ago in her unjustly neglected little book, *Helping Ourselves: Families and the Human Network*. Household tasks, including child care, were typically shared by a network of women who were in a position to make claims on each others' good will. It was precisely because this system relied on mutual trust that it worked as well as it did, according to Howell; but it was this same element of trust and mutual obligation, in all likelihood, that eventually discredited the barter system of domestic management in the minds of people who came to experience any form of personal obligation primarily as a limitation on their own freedom. To depend on others puts us under obligation to them, whereas the impersonal mechanism of the market enables us to satisfy all our obligations by the simple act of payment. The desire to escape obligation, even more than an exaggerated respect for professional expertise, explains the professionalization of domestic services formerly carried out informally and without payment. "We have grown far from a formally approved system of barter for unpaid services," Howell observed. "We wonder if it is not more civilized, more sophisticated . . . to pay for what we need. A barter system . . . must rely on human frailty and human good will."

The barter system presupposed the existence of stable

urban neighborhoods, in which long-time residents knew enough about their neighbors to trust them, to call on them for help, and to build up reciprocal obligations of their own. The proximity of relatives and in-laws, another prerequisite of any system of unpaid exchange, was another feature of such neighborhoods. As urban sociologists have often pointed out, close-knit neighborhoods, often based on a strong sense of ethnic identity, preserved some of the features of village life in the midst of large cities. Even when the household ceased to be a unit of production, it was still bound to the surrounding community by ties of mutual obligation. The "isolation of the nuclear family"—another theme of urban sociology—was qualified by neighbors' dependence on each other for all kinds of domestic services. "Isolation" was a better description of the suburban than of the urban family; and it was the rapid expansion of suburbs, beginning in the 1940s and 1950s, that finally destroyed the social patterns I have tried to sketch in here—the informal system of collective self-help that made it possible, together with the availability of domestic servants, for women to take an active part in civic culture—and inaugurated a new era in the history of women and the family. Suburban life, organized around the shopping mall rather than the neighborhood, eradicated the last vestiges of reciprocal obligation, neighborly or familial; and it is important to see that this was precisely what made it attractive. It was not just the lure of green lawns and open spaces that drew people to the suburbs but the dream of perfect freedom, of a world in which the demands of your relatives and neighbors would be vastly reduced (if not eliminated altogether) and your time would be entirely your own.

It is often said that people went to the suburbs in search of "community," as an alternative to urban anonymity. I think it was just the other way around. What they craved was complete privacy—the freedom to bring up their children without interference from intrusive relatives and neighbors, to choose their friends on the basis of mutual interests instead of physical proximity, and to organize their time without consulting the pleasure or convenience of anyone else. Suburbs appeared to institutionalize the principle of free and unlimited choice. They were designed to exclude everything not subject to choice—the job, the extended family, the enforced sociability of the city streets. Americans hoped to put all that behind them when they headed for the seclusion of the suburbs, where they were accountable, it seemed, to no one.

It was in the suburbs, much more than in the city, that women became full-time mothers and homemakers. The traditional family, so called, where the husband goes out to work and the wife stays home with the children, was not traditional at all. It was a mid-twentieth-century innovation, the product of a growing impatience with external obligations and constraints, of the equation of freedom with choice, and of tumultuous world events that made the dream of a private refuge in the suburbs more and more appealing. The idea that domestic life would provide such a refuge had a longer history, of course, but it was only in the postwar suburbs that it came close to realization. The family could plausibly be described as a "holy refuge," an "oasis far from the maddening throng," a "bastion against depersonalization and

dehumanization," a "fortress," an "island of serenity and
support and understanding in a hectic, plastic, often ava-
ricious world," only in suburbs founded on the separation of the home not merely from the workplace but from
outside influences of any kind. Domestic servants, extended family members, friends and neighbors acting as
an informal support system—all were excluded from the
middle-class suburban household, with the result that
housewives found themselves in sole possession, free at
last to arrange things exactly as they pleased.

It did not take long for this freedom to pall. By the early
sixties (if not before), the "holy refuge" of the suburban
family came to be experienced as a "comfortable concentration camp," in Betty Friedan's memorable phrase.
The Feminine Mystique, published in 1963, launched a
new wave of feminist agitation, which has changed the
American landscape far more deeply than earlier waves—
to the point where everything that took place before the
sixties is now consigned to the era of the "traditional
family." What is striking about Friedan's manifesto,
when one returns to it almost thirty years later, is the
degree to which it was dominated by the plight of suburban women. Friedan pointed out that the "explosive
movement to the suburbs"—"those ugly and endless
sprawls which are becoming a national problem"—coincided with a "great increase in the numbers of educated
women choosing to be just housewives." It did not seem
unreasonable to interpret the "postwar suburban explosion" as the product of a "mistaken choice" made by a
new generation of women who repudiated the active life
of their predecessors and saw the family as a refuge from
increasingly unmanageable conditions in the public world.

Women with "commitments outside the home," Friedan observed, were "less likely to move to the suburbs"; but such women appeared to be a dying breed. Women brought up in an earlier day, even as late as the thirties and early forties, did not regard themselves exclusively as housewives. Eighty percent of the women who graduated from Smith in the early forties, as Friedan discovered when she took a survey of her own class of 1943, "had found some way to pursue the goals that education had given them," usually in the form of "community activity" as volunteers. After the war, however, the suburbs began to attract a "new breed of women" who were "looking for sanctuary" and were "perfectly willing to fill their days with the trivia of housewifery." "Women of this kind," according to Friedan, refused "to take policy-making positions in community organizations," leaving the "really interesting volunteer jobs" to be filled by men. They justified their "resistance to serious community responsibility" on the grounds that their families took all their time. Since housework and child care did not absorb their "full capacities," however, they soon developed the symptoms familiar to students of the "problem that has no name"—chronic fatigue, boredom, loneliness, and a "nameless aching dissatisfaction" they sought to relieve with alcohol, drugs, overeating, sexual adventures, or an obsessive interest in their children.

Except that it focused on women, Friedan's book closely resembled many other accounts of suburban life, almost all of which deplored "conformity, status-seeking, [and] escape," in Friedan's words. Like many other commentators, Friedan worried about the effects of excessive maternal attention on children growing up in suburbia, especially on boys. "A subtle and devastating change," she wrote, "seems to have taken place in the character of American children." Their lives seemed empty and pointless. "Apathetic, dependent, infantile, purposeless," these children had no consuming interests or goals. There was "nothing these kids felt strongly enough about to die for." They had no ambition, no taste for competition, and no capacity for hard work or physical endurance. Accustomed to having all their wants provided for by others, they lacked "self-sufficiency." They suffered from "passivity," "softness," "muscular deterioration." Many of the young men became homosexuals, driven by an "implacable hatred for the parasitic women who keep their husbands and sons from growing up." There was a definite link, Friedan thought, "between what is happening to the women in America and increasingly overt male homosexuality." Homosexuality, which was "spreading like a murky smog over the American scene," was "no less ominous than the restless, immature self-seeking of the young women who are the aggressors in . . . early marriages." The ease with which American prisoners in Korea were brainwashed by their captors provided further evidence of a "parasitical softening" in the American character. So did the rise of the "bearded, undisciplined beat generation"—a "singularly passionless and purposeless form of adolescent rebellion." Many other observers of American life, Friedan noted, had come to the same conclusion: that "these new kids are . . . not growing up 'real.'"

One of the most discerning of these observers, Paul Goodman, brought out his *Growing Up Absurd* in 1960, just three years before the publication of *The Feminine*

Mystique. Although nobody seems to have noticed this at the time, the two books complemented each other quite closely: Each emphasized an important dimension of the problem that was ignored by the other. They agreed in their description of the problem—the difficulty of growing up in a world that made few demands on one's intelligence or strength of character. Like Friedan, Goodman regarded the emergence of the beat generation as an important symptom of the passivity and resignation that was spreading through American society. His portrait of the beats was more sympathetic than Friedan's but no less depressing. Those who called themselves beat, as Goodman saw them, had plenty of reasons for refusing to grow up into the roles they were expected to fill as adults. But their "defensive ignorance of the academic culture," together with their "cynicism and neglect of ethical and political goals," condemned their rebellion to futility. They experienced the university "as a part of the worthless organized system rather than as Newton and Virgil." Accordingly, their literary culture remained parochial and undeveloped, dependent on the illusion that it was self-sufficient and could dispense with exposure to the larger world of letters. The beats wrote for an audience too easily impressed by third-rate work, a "somewhat sickening audience because it has no objective cultural standard." Having cut themselves off from the "stream of ancient and international tradition," they tried "to make the parochial the *only* existing culture" and thus to make themselves artists by definition. But mutual admiration was a poor substitute for the kind of artistic, literary, and intellectual achievement that could be validated by objective standards. "The artist finds that he is a parochial group hero, when the reassurance that he needs, if he is diffident, is that he is a culture hero for the immortal world." The beats' characteristic expressions of mutual praise and encouragement—"It's the greatest!" "Go, man, go!"—carried little conviction. "In a milieu of resignation, where the young men think of society as a closed room in which there are no values but the rejected rat race or what they can produce out of their own guts, it is extremely hard to aim at objective truth or world culture."

According to Goodman, the beats rejected the prevailing definition of success—money, possessions, a house in the suburbs—but shared the general conviction "that society cannot be different." Having no large hopes, they could not escape the general condition of young men "growing up absurd"—apathy, disappointment, and cynicism. The root of the difficulty was that the "organized system," as Goodman called it, did "not want men"; instead it wanted hucksters, promoters, timeservers, and entertainers. It subordinated the production of useful goods and services to the sale of commodities designed to wear out quickly, to be superseded by changes in fashion, to appeal to the public's jaded appetite for novelty, or to satisfy a desire for the social status conferred by conspicuous display. Young men wanted to feel useful, but the available jobs required them to produce and market useless consumer goods, as opposed, say, to "necessary food and shelter." A young man might choose to become an auto mechanic—a seemingly useful line of work—only to find that "cars have a built-in obsolescence" and that "manufacturers do not want them to be repaired or repairable." Under these conditions, "his feelings of justification, sociability, serviceability" were likely to dissolve. It was "not surprising" if he became "cynical and time-serving, interested in a fast buck."

This kind of experience was bound to be repeated over and over again, according to Goodman, in a society that maintained its "so-called high standard of living" by turning out commodities that no one really needed. Opponents of the New Deal had pointed out the demoralizing effects of "make-work," but the whole economy now depended on work that had no other object than to keep people at work and thus to sustain the national "capacity to consume," which in turn sustained production, which sustained full employment (or an approximation of full employment)—all without reference to the intrinsic quality of the goods and services produced or the intrinsic satisfaction of the work that went into them. The vicious circle of a consumer economy made the popular perception of the workaday world as a rat race quite appropriate. Such an economy deprived young men of the kind of work they could "enthusiastically and spontaneously throw themselves into" and thus denied them any compelling incentive to grow up at all. The ideal of "having a real job that you risk your soul in" belonged to the "heroic age of capitalist enterprise." In the new world of make-work and planned obsolescence, young men could no longer believe either in the jobs they were expected to grow up into or in the country as a whole. In the past, "there was always something special in the American destiny to be proud of." The increasingly narrow identification of the American dream with the American standard of living, however, extinguished the spirit of patriotism just as effectively as the consumer economy extinguished the spirit of workmanship.

Throughout his book, Goodman repeatedly referred to the importance of "man's work" in conferring "manly independence" and a manly character. He had next to nothing to say about young women; in a book that otherwise seems as timely today as it did thirty years ago, this silence is the only feature that is likely to strike us as curiously outdated. Goodman simply assumed, without giving the matter much thought, that housekeeping and child care were useful jobs in the nature of things—the kind of jobs that promoted self-esteem and a sense of accomplishment. This was so widely understood, according to Goodman, that men themselves had begun to embrace domesticity as a "secondary but real career." The "new fatherhood" that was taking shape in the fifties, he argued, was another indication of their disenchantment with the rat race. Whereas Friedan deplored the revival of domesticity and the flight to the suburbs, Goodman saw these developments, quite erroneously I think, as an "important new effort toward community." The new suburban "settlements" devoted "time and energy to common interests." The "improvement of the child's world" led to "genuine community participation, committee meetings and lectures on psychology, concern for traffic and zoning, and even extension courses in cultural subjects to create the proper atmosphere for growing up."

At this point, Goodman's analysis badly needed a feminist corrective. Child rearing may be an honorable calling, but many women clearly found it increasingly unsatisfactory in the fifties and sixties, and it was important to understand the reasons for this—the reasons that were to make them so receptive to Friedan's attack on the "feminine mystique." Her own explanation was quite consistent with Goodman's account of the corruption of work, although she made no reference to it. She pointed out that housekeeping and child care had themselves taken on many of the telltale characteristics of make-work. Once women gave up extrafamilial interests, "housewifery expanded to fill the time available." Women lavished more attention on domestic duties than those duties really required (or than was good for children). Like much of the work men performed in the marketplace, these duties appeared to have no other purpose than to keep women busy. Child care, moreover, was important only if it was connected with larger public purposes. Goodman himself conceded the substance of this point when he noted—though only in passing—that when adults devoted themselves exclusively to the child's world, "there isn't much world for the child to grow up into in the next stage." In order for a father "to guide his growing son," it was "necessary for him to have a community of his own and be more of a man." But the same thing was surely true of women. That this obvious point should have escaped attention until Betty Friedan made it inescapable shows why the feminist revival was necessary in the first place. Without it, even the most astute analysis of the difficulties of growing up in America would remain partial and one-sided.

But Friedan's analysis was one-sided in its own right without the kind of corrective provided by Goodman. His account of the world of work should have forewarned women that they would not gain much simply by entering the work force and achieving equality with men. Once women had rejected the "feminine mystique," it was tempting to think that professional careers would solve all their problems. From the point of view of the "comfortable concentration camp," the masculine world of competitive achievement looked glamorous and exciting (just as suburban domesticity looked warm and reassuring to men disaffected with the rat race). Women accordingly began to demand access to the allegedly "creative," "fulfilling" work enjoyed by men. They did not argue simply that it was both risky and demeaning to depend entirely on a man for support. They expected professional careers to bring them emotional fulfillment. If Goodman was right, however, they would find no more meaning than men did in careers the structure of which was governed largely by the requirements of commodity production. Goodman's point was not the conventional one that most jobs involved too much drudgery and routine and thus provided an inadequate outlet for "creativity." His point was that they did not produce anything of importance and were therefore dishonorable and demoralizing. From this point of view, a career as a highly paid lawyer, advertising executive, broadcast journalist, or college professor was even more demoralizing, if it served only to maintain the "organized system," than a job as an auto mechanic, which did not even pretend to be useful. This was an argument women very much needed to hear; otherwise they too would fall into the careerist trap. They needed to be reminded that good work was useful work, not glamorous or "stimulating" or "creative" work, and that its usefulness, moreover, could not be measured by a wage or salary.

Nothing in *The Feminine Mystique* was inconsistent with such a view of work, any more than *Growing Up Ab-*

surd was incompatible with a feminist perspective on the domestic revival. One of the surprises in store for anyone who returns to Friedan's best-seller today is how little she was inclined to identify the work women ought to be doing with highly paid professional careers. She wanted women to get out of the house, but she did not necessarily want them to throw themselves into the job market. No doubt she was too quick to characterize the kind of work she had in mind as "creative," and her insistence that it should put a college education to good use reveals her lack of interest in working-class women; but at least she did not confuse "creativity" with payment. She urged women to find "work, paid or unpaid, requiring initiative, leadership and responsibility." What mattered was a "lifelong commitment," not a career as such— a commitment to "society" at that. Women had to "make their contribution not as 'housewives' but as citizens." All too often, however, they stepped "back from ... volunteer activity . . . at the very point when all that is needed is a more serious commitment." "The PTA leader won't run for the school board. The League of Women Voters' leader is afraid to move on into the rough mainstream of her political party." If Friedan preferred paid to unpaid work, on the whole, it was only because "being paid ... implies a definite commitment" and because a "no-nonsense nine-to-five job ... requires less discipline" than a more flexible schedule. Volunteer work, on the other hand, required self-discipline, dedication, and a talent for improvisation—qualities that were almost always in short supply.

Because the women's movement—the movement Friedan's book helped to launch—has repudiated volunteer work as the very epitome of female slavery, it is easy to miss her emphasis on citizenship and "commitment." In the sixties and seventies, this way of talking about women gave way to an ostensibly more radical, hardheaded idiom. Women could never be free, feminists argued, until they were able to compete with men in the job market, and successful competition appeared to require institutional reforms—affirmative action, unlimited abortion rights, a comprehensive program of day care financed by public funds—that went far beyond the modest reforms advocated by *The Feminist Mystique*. Friedan herself now takes the position that "without child care, women will never really advance in their careers." In the light of the subsequent radicalization of the women's movement, *The Feminine Mystique* is usually read (when it is read at all) as the first halting step down the road since traveled by an army of more militant women. But it may make more sense to read it, alongside Goodman's book, as an attempt to mark out a road that was later abandoned. These books addressed the same issue, at bottom, even though they approached it in different ways. The issue, in a word, was how to revive a sense of vocation in a society destitute of any sense of common purpose. Like Goodman, Friedan believed that "women, as well as men, can only find their identity in work that uses their full capacities." But neither women nor men, it seems, could find such work in the brave new world of postwar suburbia. Hailed as the fulfillment of the American dream, the suburbs had turned into an American nightmare. Perhaps the most revealing commentary on the new order of the suburbs, an order based on a strict separation between the home and the workplace and a strict division of sexual labor, was that each sex envied the lives led by the other. Men envied the domestic security supposedly enjoyed by their wives; women envied the exciting careers supposedly enjoyed by their husbands. As for their children—supposedly the ultimate beneficiaries of suburban life, whose needs the whole system was intended to serve—their aimless, pampered existence had come to be regarded as a national scandal. Goodman was not alone in his insistence that young men were growing up "without high aims and with little sense of a natural or moral community." He was not alone in observing "how one rarely one hears, even delivered unctuously, the mention of some lofty purpose." Many other critics of American society made the same observation in the late fifties and early sixties, though none explained so clearly why this absence of collective purpose made it so hard for young men to grow up. The effect of Friedan's book, considered in this context, ought to have been to discourage any lingering hope that young women were growing up any better than young men and at the same time to make it clear that the difficulties faced by women were not faced by women alone. "Why aren't girls forced to grow up?" Friedan asked. Because they had "no goal, no purpose, no ambition." But if the same thing could be said of young men, careers for women could hardly provide any more than a small part of the solution.

My purpose in saying this is not to urge women to abandon the workplace or to force them into a position of economic dependence but merely to point out that professional careers are no more liberating for women than for men if those careers are governed by the require-

ments of the corporate economy. As long as the workplace is dominated by the need to sustain economic growth
by producing goods and services no one really needs, it
will be unable to satisfy the desire to become not just self-
supporting but useful and self-respecting. Nor will the
employment of women transform the workplace, as feminists often promise. Putting women in charge of corporations, law firms, newspapers, publishing houses, TV
stations, universities, and hospitals does not make those
institutions more democratic and humane. It does not
soften the masculine drive for competitive achievement
with the feminine gift for friendly cooperation. It does
not make capitalist institutions more loving and maternal. Those institutions have a life of their own, quite independent of the qualities of the people who manage
them. They obey the laws of the market, not the golden
rule. They have only one overriding aim, to show a profitable return on investment; everything else is incidental.
Under corporate capitalism, use value will always remain secondary to exchange value. Under the economic
conditions that prevail today, the connection between
them is even more tenuous than it was in the past. Financial speculation has become far more profitable than
production, and production itself is driven by marketing
strategies that rely on the familiar technique of planned
obsolescence. Advertising, the quintessential art form in
late capitalist societies, seeks to encourage a taste for
novelty and to create dissatisfaction with anything old or
out-of-date. Its ideal is a world of disposable goods, where
things are discarded as soon as they have lost their initial
appeal. That anything should be repaired, restored, or
renewed is foreign to the advertising ethic, which in-

vokes the myth of technological progress in order to re-inforce the idea that commodities advertised as new and revolutionary, upgraded and improved, are necessarily superior to the ones they drive out of the market. Often the "improvement" is purely cosmetic, but even when it serves some purpose, it usually defeats one that is equally important. The word processor is not an unambiguous improvement over the typewriter, but it puts the typewriter out of business, just as private motor cars have replaced other forms of transportation that were better suited to certain purposes. The replacement of long-playing records by compact discs, of silent films by talkies, of ocean liners by airplanes, of midwives by obstetricians, of neighborhood stores by shopping malls, of voting by public opinion polls illustrates the same point—that new technologies and the practices that grow up around them tend to become monopolies in an economy that relies so heavily on the principle of enforced obsolescence to sustain high levels of growth. Instead of expanding the range of social and private choice, as enthusiasts of innovation constantly assert, new technologies force consumers to accept what the market dictates. The celebration of choice, another important element in the ideology of progress and consumption, obscures the restriction of choice to the latest innovations, whether or not they answer the purposes they allegedly aim to satisfy.

Women's entry into the work force does not change any of this. The feminist movement, far from civilizing corporate capitalism, has been corrupted by it. It has adopted mercantile habits of thought as its own. Its relentless propaganda against the "traditional" family is of a piece with the propaganda of commodities, which encourages the consumer to discard arrangements that are still serviceable only because they are said to lag behind the times. Like the advertising industry, the women's movement has taken "choice" as its slogan, not only in the matter of abortion but in its attack on the old-fashioned family, now held to be only one of a variety of family types among which people may freely choose. In fact, however, the movement recognizes only one choice—the family in which adults work full-time in the marketplace. Its demand for state-supported programs of day care discriminates against parents who choose to raise their own children and forces everyone to conform to the dominant pattern. Indifferent to this inequity, feminists extol the dominant pattern as the irresistible product of social developments analogous to the development of technology, which automatically renders old ways obsolete. The two-career family represents "progress," and laggards have to fall in line: Such is the logic feminists have borrowed from the marketplace without any awareness of its incompatibility with their vision of a kinder, gentler world.

Mainstream feminism is now concerned almost exclusively with a single goal—to "empower" women to enter business and the professions on an equal footing with men. Even its obsession with the abortion issue has to be seen in this light. Since the biology of reproduction is the most dramatic difference between men and women and the most important source, it appears, of women's industrial inequality, it is necessary to neutralize this "disability" by giving women absolute rights over the embryo. The assertion of "reproductive rights" removes the last obstacle to women's absorption into the work force. It is significant that the National Organization for Women (NOW) has failed to support legislation that would require employers to grant parental leaves. More-flexible work schedules are not part of its agenda. Evidently because it believes that women would take advantage of such leaves more readily than would men, NOW suspects that a parental leave policy would perpetuate the division of labor that assigns women the primary role in child care and thus inhibits their professional advancement. In the highly competitive world of business and the professions, those who stray from the careerist path pay a heavy price. Advancement depends on an early start, a willingness to work long hours, and a single-minded adherence to the prevailing standards of productivity. Those who allow their children to slow them down lose out in the race for success.

A strategy more consistent with the original aims of the feminist movement, one might imagine, would challenge the prevailing definition of success. It would challenge the separation of the home and the workplace. It would criticize the suburban ideal, as it did in the beginning. It would criticize the re-creation of suburbia in the gentrified, yuppified city—another false solution that fails to address the real issue, the segregation of home life and work life. Without advocating a return to household production, a feminism worthy of the name would insist on a closer integration between people's professional lives and their domestic lives. Instead of acquiescing in the family's subordination to the workplace, it would seek to remodel the workplace around the needs of the family. It would question the ideology of economic growth and productivity, together with the careerism it fosters. A feminist movement that respected the achievements of women in the past would not disparage housework, motherhood, or unpaid civic and neighborly services. It would not make a paycheck the only symbol of accomplishment. It would demand a system of production for use rather than profit. It would insist that people need self-respecting, honorable callings, not glamorous careers that carry high salaries but take them away from their families. Instead of seeking to integrate women into the existing structures of the capitalist economy, it would appeal to women's issues in order to make the case for a complete transformation of those structures. It would reject not only the "feminine mystique" but the mystique of technological progress and economic development. It would no longer care about showing how "progressive" it was. By rejecting "progress," of course, it would put itself beyond the pale of respectable opinion— which is to say, it would become as radical as it now merely claims to be.

THE FAMILY AND THE MODERN THEATER: REPRESENTATIONS OF CHANGE

by

Robert W. Corrigan

Robert W. Corrigan

Robert W. Corrigan is Dean of the School of Arts and Humanities and Professor of Art and Performance at The University of Texas at Dallas. He received his B.A. degree from Cornell University, his M.A. degree from Johns Hopkins University, and his Ph.D. degree from the University of Minnesota.

Dean Corrigan's peripatetic teaching and administrative career at eleven institutions includes serving as Andrew Mellon Professor and Head of the Department of Drama at Carnegie-Mellon University, the founding Dean of the School of Arts at New York University, the founding President of the California Institute of the Arts, and—for a decade before coming to U.T. Dallas in 1984—Dean of the School of Fine Arts at the University of Wisconsin-Milwaukee.

A prolific author, editor, and translator, Dean Corrigan has published over 100 articles and 38 books, including Theatre in Search of a Fix *and* The World of the Theatre. *He was the founder and first editor of* The Tulane Drama Review *(now* The Drama Review*).*

Since 1980, Dean Corrigan has made annual three-week lecture tours for the State Department. He has been Chairman of the Review Panel in Theatre & Dance & Film for the Fulbright Fellowships, Vice President of the University and College Theatre Association, a member of the National Council in the Arts (NEA), the President of the International Council of Fine Arts Deans, and the Chairman of the Board of SPACE for Innovative Development in New York City. He has been awarded three honorary degrees.

THE FAMILY AND THE MODERN THEATER: REPRESENTATIONS OF CHANGE

by

Robert W. Corrigan

In my many years in the theater, the inseparable relationship between the family and the theater has been one of my abiding concerns. So, I am honored to be given the opportunity to discuss some of the dimensions of this relationship as one of the Andrew Cecil Lecturers.

Even a cursory examination of Western drama reveals that our theater throughout history has been primarily concerned with the mysteries of being and identity. As I have written elsewhere, this explains why, at the root of almost every lasting play, there are a husband and wife, a mother and father, brother and sister and sweetheart, parents and children, lovers, friends and enemies, and their surrogates. It is the *House* of Atreus and the *House* of Laius. At the heart of most of Shakespeare's plays is the family. Think of *Hamlet, Lear, Macbeth, Othello, Romeo and Juliet.* And since Shakespeare's time we can say the same is true in the works of Racine, Ibsen, Chekhov, Strindberg, Yeats, Ionesco, Pirandello, Brecht, even Beckett. The theater's special power is to manifest familial mysteries and family conflicts, including those quarrels we have with our familial dead who continue to live within us. In the theater, it's "All in the Family"!

Our lives have their beginning, middle, and end with our families in some form, and we experience life most intensely and dramatically in this context. The theater,

163

alone of all the arts, is primarily concerned with presenting these family conflicts—and their resolutions—
in such a way that we experience their truth, ambiguity,
and mystery. The theater's fundamental concern is with
those questions that haunt our consciousness, those mysteries that are ultimately beneath all of the why's we ask
about ourselves and our lives.

What makes this inseparable link between theater and
the family so interesting is the fact that the way we give
definition to family life is in direct correspondence to
our larger view of the world as a whole. Thus, any major
shift in the way a society thinks about the family and its
role in society will sooner or later emerge in the forms
of drama. This is particularly true in times like our own,
when the patterns of familial life and behavior are changing so radically and in such a bewildering manner that
one can assert with some confidence that they reflect, as
they have in the past, a major cultural shift in consciousness. In fact, I believe that change in the ways people
think about the family not only reflects a concomitant
major shifting in consciousness but also transforms the
ways in which the arts make present the new consciousness. So theater both reflects familial change and also
uses as its basic raw materials the tensions, violence, and
conflicts of family life—conflicts that constantly put our
identity into question and also remind us of the "otherness" of the human condition.

That otherness, which is the shaping element in the psychological development of each and every one of us, is
also one of the basic premises of the theater. In fact, the
more you think of the nature of the theater event, the
more it reveals about the condition of otherness and our

experience of it and furthermore explains the ambiguity of our response to an experience based on people being someone else—the actor as other. What is the source of that sense of otherness that each of us must learn to live with? How does it enter our lives? What does it have to do with theater?

Developmental psychologists tell us that the infant's first major experience of anxiety is that moment (at six to eight months of age) when it first becomes conscious of mother as mother, that is, as someone other than the self or an extension of the self. In distinguishing between the I and the non-I, the child must confront the stranger as the other and for the first time is conscious of itself as an independent being who has, in effect, been forced to leave home. The child becomes conscious of the gap between the self and the source of life, and this sense of infantile loss is something we carry with us for the rest of our lives. "We want to go home again!" There has been a great deal of research on this subject, and this is not the occasion to do much more than introduce it. But the point to understand here is that a ghost haunts each of us from our infancy to the grave, and it comes from our first awareness of separation, our otherness. Our most significant struggles with this ghost take place within the family and within the home. The theater's greatest challenge is to present that ghost in performance. I think it is no accident that the contradictions of otherness are incorporated in the emblem by which the theater has always and everywhere been identified, the mask.

As important as the theater has been in mirroring the evolving history of the family, it has not played a major role as an agent of change. Theater reflects change and thereby enables audiences to understand more fully the conditions of change, but, with few major exceptions, it has been only a peripheral player in social change. On the other hand, the legal system, which also shares much with the theater, has always been a key agent in the process of societal change. Even a brief review of the history of the family in Western culture will reveal that profound cultural shifts are first consciously experienced in the family and that changes in both the ideas and the practice of family life are inextricably linked to the courts of law.

Changes in familial behavior and mores may at first be considered as disturbing and isolated aberrations from the commonly accepted status quo as defined by the courts. In some instances things go no further than that. But some issues just will not go away. They grow to such an extent that most sectors of the community come to believe that the existing laws (if any do exist) are out-of-date, in need of revision, inadequate, and even wrong in their judgments. This is a turbulent process, and we are going through such a process right now. We may not be conscious of the dimension of the change, but there is a growing body of evidence that these changes are becoming institutionalized by legislation (at all levels of government), decree, and legal appeal and as judgments handed down by the courts.

There is another institution that must be considered as we explore the idea of family and how it relates to theater. That institution came into play at the beginning of the eighteenth century and is still the major shaping force in our thinking about familial life. I am referring to the idea of "home." We never think of "home" when we think of the Greeks and Romans, the Middle Ages, or the Renaissance. Rather, we think about kingdoms and palaces and castles. We seldom see how people lived outside the palace. We are not prompted to wonder about the plumbing. Above all, life in those castles in all its aspects was public. The Middle Ages had no concept of either physical comfort or privacy. Try to imagine yourself into *Macbeth*, running around Inverness, upstairs and downstairs, in the midst of garbage and muck. People (including kings) lived publicly. They met, talked, slept, made love, bathed, ate, drank, and murdered in the same rooms. Home, on the other hand, connotes the idea of interior life. It is based on the ideas and the ideals of privacy, intimacy, interiority, domesticity, comfort, and, perhaps most important, personal ownership. Home is a family place in which the public and the private are clearly distinguished. It was not until the eighteenth century that the home was thought of as a place of physical well-being, enjoyment, coziness, and comfort. This definition of home emerged with the rising middle class. It is this world that was later described in the writings of Jane Austen, Sir Walter Scott, and Anthony Trollope. Home is a phenomenon and product of the bourgeois age. It is both a physical place *and* a state of being. "A house is not a home," as Polly Adler, the notorious New York madam, reminded us. A house is a building; home is where we live, where we have "all the comforts of home." We speak of "going home," not "going house." Home brings together house and households, dwelling and refuge, ownership and affection. Home also brings the children together to live and be educated.

As part of these changes there emerged a most im-

portant character: The Homemaker. Enter the mother—
and this led to the feminization of the home. As Witold
Rybczynski wrote in his important little book *Home: A
Short History of an Idea*:

> "Ever since the 17th century, when privacy was in-
> troduced into the homes, the role of women in defin-
> ing comfort has been paramount. The Dutch interior,
> the Rococo Salon, the servantless household—all
> were the result of woman's incentive. One could ar-
> gue, with only slight exaggeration, that the idea of
> domesticity was principally a feminine idea. So was
> the idea of efficiency." (Viking, 1986, p. 223.)

This marked the era of bourgeois modernism and the
eventual supremacy of romanticism. For reasons we need
not bother with here, the theater was not particularly responsive to the impulses generated by the new middle
class, and the theater as a serious art form was in eclipse
throughout the eighteenth century.

It was not until the emergence of Ibsen, Strindberg,
and Chekhov in the last third of the nineteenth century
that the theater was again a significant art form. The
revolutionary plays of Ibsen and the other giants of modern theater are rooted in familial conflicts taking place
within the home. But there was something different
about these new plays. The domestic locale of the great
naturalistic plays was the living room. Battles were now
fought in the living room, not on the fields of Agincourt.
This represents a shift of great significance. As I said
earlier, whenever there are radical changes in the way
human action is represented on the stage, it is an indica-

tion that they reflect corresponding changes in the world outside the theater. A new theater comes into being. We have a new stage, a new theatrical cosmos that opens up a new vision of the world. To say "all the world's a stage" implies a governing cosmology and its attending metaphysics. Never has this been more apparent than in the bourgeois naturalistic theater of the past 150 years.

Beginning with Ibsen, the themes of the new theater were increasingly interiorized as playwrights sought to dramatize the psychic conflicts of their characters. More and more women were the protagonists of the plays. Ibsen gave us Nora Helmer (*A Doll's House*), Mrs. Alving (*Ghosts*), Rebecca West (*Rosmersholm*), Hedda Gabler (*Hedda Gabler*), Hilda Wangel (*The Master Builder*); Strindberg gave us Laura (*The Father*), Julie (*Miss Julie*), Alice (*Dance of Death*); and Chekhov in particular created complex female characters—Irina and Nina (*The Sea Gull*), Yelena and Sonya (*Uncle Vanya*), Olga, Masha, Irina, and Natasha (*Three Sisters*), and Madame Arkadina (*The Cherry Orchard*). Acting styles became more natural, and the actors worked in a more natural setting on stage, rather than standing around the prompt box. Decor and properties had to be authentic. The nature of language became more conversational; indeed the structure of many of these plays was a series of conversations—just like at home. And the subject matter became contemporary. In short, unquestionably the most creative period in the theater since Shakespeare's and Moliere's in the seventeenth century derived from the energies, values, customs, and styles of the middle-class family. The solid and stolid living room is the center of the bourgeois world.

In the twentieth century, this world was somehow to survive two world wars and a depression. Then everything began to change. The placidity and self-satisfaction of the 1950s, which several of my colleagues describe elsewhere in this volume, actually masked the turmoil that would begin to reveal itself in the 1960s and 1970s. We can see today that it was a period of real revolution. It began with the civil rights movement in the 1950s and soon grew to encompass militant concern for the environment, the banning of nuclear weapons, advocacy for female and gay liberation, and a determination to put an end to the Vietnam War. It was a time of revolution in the arts as well, and this was particularly so in the theater. It was the era of happenings and participatory performance. Plays moved off the stage out into the streets, garages, and fields, and everyone was a performing self. In short, everything was breaking down and breaking out. The theater, like all the other arts, was in a state of upheaval. The makers of the new theater failed to realize many of their lofty aspirations, but they accomplished one all-important thing: They revealed how inadequate for our times the vision, the language, and the structures of the traditional theater were. It now seems clear that most of our talented and innovative young artists sensed this inadequacy, and as a result, the most interesting theater of the past decades is largely the fruit of their efforts to deal with the growing awareness that our culture was going through a profound transformation of consciousness.

Finally, we should emphasize that what started in the 1950s and 1960s as an examination of the relation of art to life, in the hopes of making the arts more relevant, soon became primarily concerned with the expanding of consciousness. There has been a growing awareness that the basic premises of our industrial/urban culture are breaking down or not working. Or to put it more positively, we are becoming increasingly conscious of the fact that reality as we are experiencing it cannot be adequately expressed and dealt with by the structures of the past. As we try to come to terms with changes, the expansion of individual consciousness has become the focus for much of American life and culture for at least the past decade. Certainly the theater has not been exempt. Nor have the composition and practices of family life. In fact, because there has always been such a great affinity between the family and the theater, raising these questions will, I hope, point the way we must take if we are to understand the transformation of the contemporary family.

Today, whenever we talk about the family, the thorniest problem we face is defining just what a family is. It used to be very simple: The family was comprised of a married couple, one a male, the other a female, and their minor children living together in a common residence. The father was the head of the household, the mother was the helpmate, and the children went to school. Marriage was believed to be a lifelong commitment, and sex was confined to marriage. What a far cry this is from today, when there is mounting evidence of the need for a wider definition of a family. I suppose we could say that a family is any grouping of two or more people domiciled together. But that formulation is too general and too simple to deal with ever-growing and sophisticated distinctions. Let me mention just a few of the easier ones. By the year 2000, step-families will outnumber all other types combined. Gay/lesbian marriage is increasingly recognized by custom, by churches, and by law in some cities, and many of these partnerships involve children, both natural and adopted. In the past few years, family has gradually been redefined to encompass any group of people living together, including such variations as single parents and children, unmarried couples, and gay/lesbian couples. The problems related to these combinations are just beginning to surface, and quite frankly the courts have had a nearly impossible job of defining in legal terms that psychological and economic unit called a family. In fact, the law is basically trying to catch up to these transformations in contemporary family structures.

A good example of this may be found in the case of *Stahl, Inc. v. Braschi* from the summer of 1990. In this case, New York's highest court, the New York State Court of Appeals, expanded the legal definition of family, holding that a gay couple who had lived together for a decade could be considered a family under New York City's rent-control regulation. One of the couple had died in 1986, and the owners of the building sought to evict the surviving partner, claiming that family rights did not exist and therefore could not be passed on. The court, in a 4 to 2 decision, ruled otherwise as follows:

> "Protection against eviction should not rest on fictitious legal distinctions or genetic history, but instead should find its foundation in the reality of family life. In the context of eviction a more realistic, and certainly equally valid, view of a family includes two adult lifetime partners whose relationship is long-term and characterized by an emotional and finan-

cial commitment and interdependence." (Quoted in *The New York Times*, July 6, 1990.)

Later the court called for the establishment of a "new test for determining what kind of relationship qualifies as a family." The factors that the judges said should be considered included these:

Exclusivity and longevity of a relationship;
The level of emotional and financial commitment;
How a couple has conducted their everyday lives and held themselves out to society;
The reliance placed upon one another for daily family services.

The majority opinion concluded, "It is the totality of the relationship as evidenced by the dedication, caring and self-sacrifice of the parties which should, in the final analysis, control." Who is capable of making such judgments?

Numerous other issues are just as ambiguous as those raised by the *Braschi* case, if not more so. As they slowly get resolved, it is almost a certainty that family law will be drastically changed. Indeed, one could further argue that more changes, if they are realized, will in all probability transform the very ethical and moral foundations upon which our society is based. Think of the ramifications of just a few of the moral/family issues that will confront our society in the next decade:

Euthanasia and the individual's right to die.
Legal rights of children, grandparents, and even pets.

The homeless and the family—what does the grow-
ing number of the homeless tell us about the home?
Abortion: pro-choice vs. pro-life.
Surrogate births.
Reproductive technology.
Individual vs. family rights.
Demographic change.

All of these issues have become entangled in our legal
system and are likely to continue there as society searches
for answers. Let me make a few comments on just two
of these issues: demographic change and reproductive
technology.

First, however, let me tell you of a funny little tidbit
that I found as I scanned the newspapers for esoterica on
family life. What state has the largest number of out-of-
state adoptions? Iowa! Iowa is having an adoption boom—
everyone wants to adopt babies from Iowa. This boom is
explained by a professor of family law at Drake University who said, "Prospective parents see Iowa as a source
of 'country fresh girls' and 'farm fresh babies.'"

Let me now say a few words about the effects of new
demographics on our family life. Unquestionably, changing demographics are reshaping all of American life.
In the past two decades, the ethnic profile has changed
radically and will continue to do so. In the process, it
will change the definition of the American family. "Today, ethnicity has replaced assimilation," wrote Arthur
Schlesinger, Jr., in 1990 in a very interesting and pro-
vocative article published in the *Wall Street Journal*. He
stresses that a basic shift has occurred and that a new
national ethos is emerging:

"These developments portend a new turn in American life. Instead of a transformative nation with a new and distinctive identity, America increasingly sees itself as a preservative of old identities. We used to say *e pluribus unum*. Now we glorify *pluribus* and belittle *unum*. The melting pot yields to the Tower of Babel." ("When Ethnic Studies Are Un-American," *Wall Street Journal*, June 21, 1990, p. A14, col. 3.)

This shift has led to what has been called "a new tribalism," an idea discussed in an article in *The New York Times* by Richard Bernstein:

"Today in New York there are probably more foreign-born residents than there were in the 1930s. The city has something like 60 foreign-language newspapers. Across the country, in Los Angeles, more than half of the children in the public school system are Hispanic. Nearly 30 percent of the incoming freshmen in the vast University of California system are Asians. A new immigration law being considered by Congress now would allow 750,000 people into the country each year." ("The Arts Catch Up With a Society in Disarray," *The New York Times*, September 2, 1990, Sec. 2, p. H1, col. 1.)

What is rapidly becoming a global migration challenges our old, comfortable definitions of family as we become less and less Western in our ethnic and cultural makeup.

Let me take one more example—almost an absurd example—to show you the quandary society finds itself in as we struggle with the definition of family in an era of advanced reproductive technology. I refer to the *Davis v. Davis* case in Tennessee. The subject is, "Who owns the frozen embryos?" Sensing that this would be a significant story, *The New York Times* followed it in great detail. Briefly the Davises' story goes something like this:

> "Having been unable to conceive a child, they [the Davises] had turned to *in vitro* fertilization, a process in which eggs are extracted surgically from a woman's body and mixed with sperm in a laboratory dish. Those that are fertilized can be implanted in the womb." (*The New York Times*, May 26, 1990.)

Several months later, without having successfully implanted the embryo, the couple got a divorce. The basic dispute of which party gets the embryos arose. Again, I quote:

> "In his decision, the judge held that 'human life begins at the moment of conception and that the issue was therefore the best interest of the child,' just as Mrs. Stowe [both Davises had since remarried] had contended. Mr. Davis, who had argued that the issue was really one of joint property and that he should not be forced to become a parent, appealed to the Tennessee Court of Appeals. Mrs. Stowe claimed she wanted to have a baby with the embryos."

Mrs. Stowe subsequently decided she did not want to implant the embryo created with her original husband.

She wanted the authority to give the embryos to another childless couple. Mr. Davis responded, "There is just no way I am going to donate them. I feel that's my right. If there was a child from them, then I would be a parent to it. And I don't want a child out there to be mine if I can't be a parent to it." He further argued that this was a joint property issue and that if one of the embryos were used by anyone else, he would be made a parent against his will and would be legally responsible for child support. In the meantime, who is protecting the best interests of the embryos? Up steps a lawyer:

> " 'Since the judge has ruled that the embryos are life or persons, then somebody needs to represent their best interests,' said lawyer R. D. Hash. 'It's unclear to me if either parent really wants them, so they are truly orphans. Medical personnel say the shelf life of embryos is two years, so if they are to have a chance to survive, somebody needs to act quickly.' " (*The Dallas Morning News*, July 29, 1990.)

Finally the case got to the Tennessee Court of Appeals, but Tennessee does not have any laws pertaining to "the ownership of frozen embryos." The court with Solomon-esque wisdom ruled that "Mrs. Stowe and Mr. Davis should both share an interest in the seven fertilized ova." (*The Dallas Morning News*, September 11, 1990.) Mrs. Davis has not yet decided whether to pursue the case in the Tennessee Supreme Court. No matter, because whatever she does will be moot, since at the time of this writing the embryos are now twenty-two months old, and, as you recall, a frozen embryo has a "shelf life" of two years. A bizarre story, but not so unusual when one begins to look at news items with the family in mind.

I bring my remarks to a close by stressing the fact that I am not calling for more plays to deal with the family in the contemporary world. One cannot legislate or predict what playwrights choose to treat. In the past two decades, many plays, some of them quite good, have been written with the family at the center. I think of Pinter (*The Birthday Party*, *The Homecoming*), Mamet (*American Buffalo*), Cristofer (*Shadow Box*), Churchill (*Cloud Nine*), Akalaitis (*Green Card*), Terry (*Keep Tightly Closed in a Cool Place*), Wasserstein (*The Heidi Chronicles*), and Shepard (especially *Buried Child*, which in my view is one of the first postmodern dramas, if there is such a thing). Rather, I am observing that in this period of turbulent change, we need a new or greatly revised legal system that will reflect the oftentimes painful changes in our thinking and behavior in relation to the family and the home. This is easier said than done. New laws represent new concepts of responsibility, they create new questions, and they raise still other unexpected issues. New laws force us to face "choice" in a universe of ambiguous and unstable values. But without them, there can be no judgments, judgments that bring order, distinction, and meaning to both life and art.

So, how to end? This is and always has been the central issue of a dramatic action, and today it is the biggest problem facing not only our theater but our society as well. I have written elsewhere that the dramatic actions of theater have both a teleological and an eschatological basis—teleological in that they affirm that in nature a design or purpose exists and can be known and also that phenomena not only are guided by outside forces but move toward certain final causes and goals of self-realization, in short, that action moves to endings; and eschatological in that they affirm that this movement will be realized in a final end and with a judgment. We seem to be living in a world that lacks a form and meaning that an end implies. Our deep need for intelligible ends does not as yet correspond to our perceptions of the emerging new paradigms of thought and experience that will shape the ways we make sense of the world. This condition makes it difficult to think much about ends and endings. But one thing is clear: As our sense of the end changes (or has changed), so also do those relationships that lead to an end. And the contemporary theater's solipsistic obsession with its own processes reveals its dilemma. Having no well-defined sense of an end, process becomes an end in itself.

However, this is neither satisfying nor fulfilling—not in the theater, not in the courts. My dissatisfaction with postmodern theater is not with its images or its style but with its lack of a recognizable and experienced teleology. As I look back over the recorded history of Western theater, I find that in its most significant and powerful manifestations, its central subject has been the family, its central structure has been teleological, and the central need in audiences that it has fulfilled is our need to have dramatic representation of our familial conflicts brought to a meaningful end in judgment. More and more today I sense that, together with Kent in *King Lear*, we ask, "Is this the promis'd end?" A dramatic action presupposes and requires that an end will bestow upon the whole an

orderly duration and a meaning. A dramatic action presupposes and requires that our perception of the present, memory of the past, and expectations of the future
can exist in a common and unified structure. A dramatic
action presupposes and requires that our concerns over
our individual end in death and the ends or purposes
of the world can be represented in such a manner that
they are consonant with their beginnings and in such a
way that all of the stages from beginning to end are in
concord.

In another Cecil Lecture this year, Professor Glendon
makes a persuasive case that we should not think of families without thinking about what they are connected to.
She refers to the many new networks that are coming into
being—networks that are so supportive and strengthen-
ing that it is possible to entertain the notion that there
can be an ecology of family life that is more responsive to
our familial needs than are the structures of the nuclear
family that seem so inadequate today. The idea of ecological networks as a viable familial structure is an
intriguing one, and that such a structure exists is con-
firmed by the many ways we are re-creating a sense of
community and familial sharing through these networks. Professor Glendon uses the term "connections."
For me the key term or idea—as Frank Kermode demonstrated so eloquently in his book *The Sense of an Ending*—
is *concord*. It affirms that there can be a consonance between our imaginative structures and the daily lives we
lead. It reaffirms the possibility of meaningful correspondence in the world, even as it acknowledges that
there will always be a tension between paradigmatic
form and contingent reality.

So, finally, I come to the end. The challenge facing those who would reintegrate the centrality of the family to the rest of our life and being is to discover those consonances that exist in the new paradigms that are emerging in our postmodern world. The challenge is to discover the forms that will give shape and meaning to our lives as we live them. To meet the challenge both in and out of the theater is to search for new endings. Several years ago, President Francois Mitterand of France convened an international conference to discuss "Creation and Development." He closed his welcoming address to the assembly of artists, scientists, philosophers, and other intellectuals as follows:

> "Today, as yesterday, disorder must give rise to a higher order. From the absence of meaning must appear a new design. Our task, your task, is to invent new endings—a civilization of work no longer separated from life, nor from the spirit, but which makes man whole, even on the level of his daily life."

MICHAEL JORDAN

MICHAEL JORDAN

Basketball's Soaring Star

Paul J. Deegan

Lerner Publications Company ■ Minneapolis

This book is available in two editions:
Library binding by Lerner Publications Company
Soft cover by First Avenue Editions
241 First Avenue North
Minneapolis, Minnesota 55401

To Dorothy, my best friend

LIBRARY OF CONGRESS CATALOGING-IN-PUBLICATION DATA

Deegan, Paul J. 1937-
  Michael Jordan: basketball's soaring star.
  (The Achievers)
  Summary: Describes the life and career of the Chicago
Bulls basketball player who became the first player in
twenty-four years to score more than 3,000 points in one
season.
  1. Jordan, Michael, 1963-   —Juvenile literature. 2.
Basketball players—United States—Biography—Juvenile
literature. 3. Chicago Bulls (Basketball team)—Juvenile
literature. [1. Jordan, Michael, 1963-   . 2. Basketball
players. 3. Afro-Americans—Biography] I. Title. II. Series.
GV884.J67D44   1988   796.32'3'0924 [B] [92]   87-29669
ISBN 0-8225-0492-8 (lib. bdg.)
ISBN 0-8225-9548-6 (pbk.)

Copyright © 1988 by Lerner Publications Company

Manufactured in the United States of America

International Standard Book Number: 0-8225-0492-8 (lib. bdg.)
International Standard Book Number: 0-8225-9548-6 (pbk.)
Library of Congress Catalog Card Number: 87-29669

    5 6 7 8 9 10 98 97 96 95 94 93 92 91 90

921
Jor

Contents

150158

1

Records Lead to Recognition

One of the most exciting scenes in sports today is basketball player Michael Jordan of the Chicago Bulls preparing to shoot a basket. Ball in hand, eyes narrowed in concentration, his tongue hanging out, Jordan becomes a devastating weapon. He can dart past a defensive player in a flash or outjump him and score the basket. His speed and jumping ability are just two of Jordan's many assets, which include his size, strength, control, large hands, and durability. The 6-foot, 6-inch guard with the acrobatic leaping ability is fast on his way to becoming one of the all-time greats of the National Basketball Association (NBA).

Michael Jordan is considered one of the best players in the NBA today. During the 1986–87 season, he scored 3,041 points, the third highest total in NBA history after Wilt Chamberlain's two highest scoring totals. Jordan was the first player in 24 years to score more than 3,000 points in one season. Until Jordan averaged 37.1 points a game in the 1986–87 regular season, no NBA guard had ever averaged more than 34 points in a game.

Bobby Knight, considered one of the country's most successful college coaches, called Jordan one of the two best college players he's seen in the last 10 years. Larry Bird, the Boston Celtics' famous forward and three-time NBA Most-Valuable-Player award winner, said Jordan "can do things that nobody else does in this league. He's got everything."

Many people think Bird is the best player in basketball today. But Bird says, "Jordan can do a lot of things that I can't do. I can't jump like him. I can't run like him. I can't just go over people to get to the bucket. Never seen anyone like him. Phenomenal. One of a kind. He's the best ever."

Jordan makes it seem simple. He says the moves for which he is becoming famous in arenas across the country are spontaneous. "The special shots are alternatives after the defense makes me change the normal shot," Jordan has said. "I can't plan what I'm doing because I don't know what the defender is going to do."

That spontaneity makes Jordan a tough opponent. A defensive player has no idea what Jordan might do next. His many abilities make him hard to defend against.

Even when defenses make him change his shot, Jordan has a knack for getting the ball off in traffic.

Jordan's very large hands, which can wrap a basketball, are an
asset to him on the court.

At 195 to 200 pounds, he is very strong and is not easily bumped around. His great body control and agility enable him to shoot successfully in tight situations.

Jordan's very large hands make it easy for him to control the ball, switch the ball from hand to hand, and grasp the ball firmly when he flies toward the hoop. His large hands also allow him to fake a pass, then pull the ball back and bypass a defender.

Many observers have noted Jordan's almost uncanny ability to stay in the air for a long time when he leaps for a basket. Basketball players call this time in the air "hang time." Jordan appears at times to hang forever. One reporter said that Jordan "seems to float in midair and wait for other men to fall to earth before he shoots."

Jordan's first coach with the Bulls, Kevin Loughery, compared Jordan's hang time to that of all-time NBA great Julius Erving—"Dr. J." "Players with great hang time," Loughery said, "can stay up there when they jump in the air." He added that they can "get their bodies into different positions in the air."

Erving, after playing against Jordan for the first time, said, "In some ways, it's like looking into a mirror." Erving called Jordan's playing "something magical or mystical." Jordan said he was flattered to be compared with Dr. J, but he added, "He [Erving] made his own footsteps, and I don't want to follow in his. I want to make my own—size 13."

After opponents drop out of his way, Jordan, still in midair, is often able to score.

Jordan shares one physical skill with nearly all other great athletes—foot speed and overall quickness. Jordan's powerful first step catapults him into his remarkable drives to the basket, often followed by a slam dunk. Most players at the major college and professional levels can dunk the ball, but Jordan can do it by leaping higher than a 7-foot player is able to. It takes tremendous strength to jump higher than players six inches taller can jump.

The mere presence and personality of a player like Jordan lend a special quality to a basketball game. Stan Albeck, Loughery's successor as the Bulls' coach, said, "It's not only his scoring, it's his presence. He makes everyone play harder. He gets the crowd—everyone—involved." One observer of the Bulls said Jordan's ability sometimes made team members "believe they were better than they really were."

Jordan has also proved durable, playing despite colds, flu, and other nagging pains that plague a player during the six-month NBA season. Chicago assistant coach John Bach said, "That's what makes it so nice to be with the Air Jordan airline. It flies every night."

The ability to inspire teammates and durability are important, but in the end it's Jordan's great physical talent that is so exciting. Professional athletes are not easily impressed, but even NBA players admire Jordan. "Leave him alone. He's God's child," a Bulls' teammate told reporters.

Jordan's powerful first step, here moving him past the Boston
Celtics' Kevin McHale, often frees him for a slam dunk (right).

Jordan is modest about his abilities. "It's all spur-of-the-moment," he said. "If I'm in a situation where I have to do something spectacular to get out of trouble, I do it. The new moves come in as they come. It's nothing that I think about before I do it. Sometimes I don't know exactly what to do, but I end up doing it."

His talents are readily acknowledged by many in the sports world, though. Former Notre Dame star Orlando Woolridge entered the NBA three years before Jordan. Woolridge said that several elements distinguish an excellent player. "You look to see what type of things he can do instinctively, what his natural ability is, and what types of things he can do in certain pressure situations. It's easy to judge who's a good shooter, who's a good defender, who rebounds well," Woodridge said. "But a player who can do all those things, especially in pressure situations, is the type of player I look for." Woolridge said he was talking about a player "who can do the whole thing," one "with pure natural ability. A man like Michael Jordan."

2

Overcoming Disappointment

Jordan didn't begin his basketball career with the ability to do "the whole thing," however. Reaching basketball stardom was not a smooth, uninterrupted climb. His success reflects a pattern of growth that developed gradually—both on and off the basketball court. The heart of Jordan's story centers on how he succeeded in combining his strong competitive instinct with his emerging physical talent—a talent that was not so evident when he began playing high school basketball. Even after three years in one of the most successful college basketball programs in the country, no one expected Jordan to become the red-hot NBA property he is today.

Jordan committed himself to basketball only after it disappointed him. Although he had begun playing basketball as a child at an eight-foot-high basket in his backyard, his athletic skills were not obvious in his first years at Laney High School in Wilmington, North Carolina. As a sophomore at Laney in 1979, he averaged 25 points a game on the junior varsity team, and he expected a promotion to the varsity team. It never came.

Jordan responded by meeting the challenge. "The way it is in our family," his father said, "is that we try to make something happen rather than waiting around for it to happen. We believe the surest way is to work toward making it the way you want."

During the summer of 1979, Jordan turned himself into a "gym rat," practicing basketball for hours at a time. He even cut back on baseball, which had been his favorite sport, to devote more time to improving his basketball game.

His persistence paid off. Jordan made the varsity basketball team, and, by the time he was a senior, he'd become a strong player. He was no nationally sought-after schoolboy star, though. He was just one of many good high school basketball players in North Carolina. Most of his advisers urged Jordan to attend a small college in North Carolina where, they thought, he'd have more opportunity to play. Jordan saw the situation as another challenge. He chose to go to the University of North Carolina at Chapel Hill and try to succeed in one of the best major college basketball programs in the country.

Jordan began playing basketball at a basket only 8 feet high.
Now he plays above the rim of the regulation 10-foot-high basket.

And succeed he did as his growth continued. Coach Dean Smith said Jordan's progress at North Carolina was "eerie." During Jordan's three seasons with the Tar Heels, he became much more than just an average college player—he became an exceptional college player.

North Carolina Coach Dean Smith

As a college player, Jordan is best remembered for one shot he made in his first season at North Carolina. He made a 16-foot shot in the closing seconds of the 1982 National Collegiate Athletic Association (NCAA) championship game. The freshman's successful shot gave the Tar Heels a 63–62 win over Georgetown University.

A few years later, Jordan told a reporter that the 1982 championship game was his one "memorable game," noting that "everything started with my [winning] shot. That's the game I will always remember because that's when Michael Jordan got his name and started to get the respect of everyone else."

Jordan was named an All-American player and College Player of the Year in his sophomore and junior years. In his sophomore year, the Tar Heels went as far as the regional final before falling to the University of Georgia, 82–77. Jordan—listed then and the following year as 6 feet, 5 inches tall—averaged 19.1 points on 53.5 percent field-goal shooting in 1982–83. He scored 687 points and had over five rebounds a game.

As a junior in his final year at Chapel Hill, Jordan led the Atlantic Coast Conference (ACC) in scoring as North Carolina went undefeated in the conference. For the season, he averaged 19.6 points a game, making 55 percent of his field-goal attempts. Seventy-eight percent of his free throws were successful. He scored 607 points and averaged over five rebounds per game. The team's bid for another NCAA title ended in a regional semifinal game that Indiana University won, 72–68.

At Chapel Hill, Jordan learned something about basketball fans. He realized that they expected great things of him. "They're going to want me to [spin] 360 [degrees] each time I've got the ball," Jordan said. "But [now] I know if I just go out and play naturally, the people are going to be pleased." At the beginning of his final season at Chapel Hill, he said he was "trying to do it for the crowd." But he wasn't playing well. Coach Smith then showed him films of games from the previous year. "The difference was incredible," Jordan said. "From that point on, I just settled down and started to play the way I normally do, and it worked out."

Despite Jordan's impressive college record, there was still no indication of how much he would affect the NBA—an entire league of outstanding players. In particular, Jordan did not often display his unique aerial abilities at North Carolina because coach Smith's carefully constructed offensive plans did not emphasize an individual player's physical talents.

As a member and co-captain of the 1984 United States Olympic basketball team, Jordan played for a coach with a similar offensive approach. Indiana University coach Bobby Knight was not about to let a member of his team show off on the court.

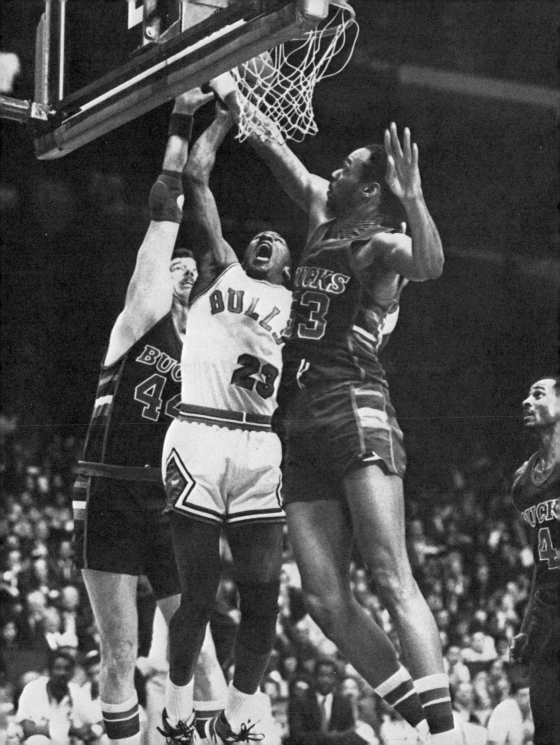

Orlando Woolridge, Jordan's Chicago Bulls team-mate, compared playing college sports to playing in an orchestra: The coach is the conductor, and players must play the music according to the coach's directions. "If you don't play the right notes, you sit down," Woolridge said. "When you get to the pros," he continued, "it's more like jazz. . . . You can just play and let your rhythm flow, do the things that come naturally and let your talent show." Coach Knight wasn't conducting jazz. However, Jordan did average just over 17 points a game in the Olympics as he led the U.S. team to a gold medal in Los Angeles.

A coach's style can limit a college player's flair. Still, Michael Jordan of the Bulls is a much more explosive player than the Michael Jordan of North Carolina and Olympic days. Jordan thinks it just took time for him to hit his stride. "In college the natural skills and ability were there, but it was a learning experience for me," he noted. "At the pro level . . . all my knowledge and ability just came together. I came to a team where the situation gave me an opportunity to show the world what I can do as a player."

In 1987, he told a reporter that "the NBA is an educational playground. It's allowed me to combine all I've learned about fundamentals with my natural skills." That combination, along with his strong competitive drive, produced immediate results when Jordan entered the NBA.

24

The decision to go to North Carolina may have seemed risky, but it worked out well for both Jordan and the University's basketball program. Although Jordan left school after his junior year for the challenges and riches of professional basketball, he also returned to college periodically and received his degree in 1986.

Chicago Bulls' ex-coach Doug Collins has expressed surprise at Jordan's ability to maintain "mountains of freshness."

3

The Jordan Family

Growing up in Wilmington, North Carolina, Jordan often felt unpopular and awkward. Although admired today by many fans, as a boy Jordan was convinced he was so ugly that he would never get married. Other kids made fun of him, and, when he got to high school, he rarely dated.

Despite his lack of self-confidence as an adolescent, Jordan today shows a healthy personality that stems from the warmth and care given to him by his family. Through their encouragement, he was able to develop the strength necessary to succeed on and off the basketball court. Today Jordan is himself both a husband and a father. In September 1989, Jordan married Juanita Vanoy, and the couple has a young son named Jeffrey.

Michael Jordan was born in Brooklyn, New York, on February 17, 1963. Shortly after his birth, his parents,

James and Dolores Jordan, moved their family to Wallace, North Carolina, James' hometown. Michael, the second youngest of five children, had two brothers and two sisters. When he was seven years old, the family moved to Wilmington. James was a plant supervisor for General Electric, and Dolores worked in public relations for a banking firm.

A friend of the family describes Dolores Jordan as "the strong one in the family" and "the disciplinarian, the steadying influence." Michael says his mother is "the one who always told me to respect my elders." Michael's father is called "fun-loving and easygoing," with "a streak of mischief that you also can see in Michael." He is also "a man who lives by the work ethic."

When Michael was young, his brothers enjoyed working with cars, appliances, radios—things they could fix. Michael, though not mechanically inclined, watched his father repair many things in their garage workshop. In those work sessions Michael picked up the habit of letting his tongue hang out while concentrating, as he saw his father do.

Michael also helped his mother in the kitchen. Since he was sure no one would marry him, he decided that he should be able to take care of himself so he could live alone someday. He asked his mother to teach him to cook, to wash clothes, to clean house, and to sew. Jordan says he was "lazy about some things" when he was growing up. "I never got into mowing the lawn or doing hard jobs. But I wasn't careless."

Dolores and James encouraged their children to excel at whatever they did. "My parents warned me about the traps [in life]," Jordan says, "the drugs, and the drink, the streets that could catch you if you got careless." Although his parents did not push Jordan toward athletics, he participated in baseball, football, and track. He says he was "trying to find the right place for my talents."

He liked baseball the most when he was growing up. "My favorite childhood memory, my greatest accomplishment," Jordan told a reporter, "was when I got the most-valuable-player award when my Babe Ruth team won the state baseball championship. That was the first big thing I accomplished in my life, and you always remember the first." Jordan treasures that championship even more than the NCAA title his North Carolina team won.

James Jordan says Michael's competitive drive comes from his mother. Michael's urge to compete extends beyond the basketball court. He hates to lose—at anything.

Jordan is competitive, but he can be warm and caring as well. He tries to be fair. During training camp for the Bulls in 1985, on a day off, Jordan began shooting pool. He played with anyone who would challenge him—five dollars a game. He beat everyone and was having a good time. He talked and laughed and jived as he played his shots, which intimidated some opponents.

One 10-year-old boy was more confident, however. The youngster, an unusually keen sharpshooter, was holding his own in a close game with Jordan. Jordan won. When Jordan asked for the five dollars, the boy lowered his head and dug into his pocket. He'd obviously thought that Jordan wouldn't make him pay if he lost. But Jordan told the boy that if he were going to gamble in life, he'd better be willing to pay the price when he lost.

Then during the next game, Jordan asked the boy to rack the balls for him, offering him five dollars to do it. The youngster seemed to appreciate the opportunity to earn back his losses, and he walked away with a smile. His faith in the fairness of a sports hero had deepened.

Tongue out, Jordan soars to the basket.

4

Jordan and the NBA

In the spring of 1984, Jordan was the first-round choice of the Chicago Bulls, the third player picked in the NBA draft. That fall, Jordan got off to an outstanding start with the Bulls, scoring 22 points in one quarter during his third regular-season game and totaling 45 points in his ninth NBA game. Chicago won three straight games on the road for the first time in three years.

Playing in every one of the Bulls' 82 regular-season games in 1984–85, Jordan led Chicago into the play-offs for the first time in four seasons. They met the central division champion, the Milwaukee Bucks, in the first round of the play-offs and were eliminated three games to one.

Jordan's scoring average of 28.2 points a game was third best in the NBA behind established stars Bernard

Bernard King of the New York Knickerbockers averaged 32.9 points per game to lead the NBA in scoring in 1984-85. He missed almost all of the next 2 seasons after suffering a devastating knee injury in March, 1985. The 6-foot, 7-inch forward was traded to the Washington Bullets just before the 1986-87 season.

King of the New York Knickerbockers and the Celtics' Larry Bird. While scoring 2,313 points, Jordan made over half of his field-goal attempts. His 2.39 steals a game was fourth best in the league.

One basketball publication asked, "Could anyone have done more in his rookie year?" His performance brought Jordan NBA Rookie-of-the-Year honors and a spot on the all-NBA team. A television announcer said Jordan "did everything except make the wind stop blowing in Chicago." He received 74 percent of the votes cast for Rookie of the Year and was named NBA Pivotal Player of the Year, an award that rates a player's overall value to his team.

The rookie Jordan also revitalized the Chicago Bulls' organization. Thousands of fans lined up to see Jordan. During games, they waited eagerly for him to make a move to the basket. With his tongue hanging out, he would soar to the basket. The fans loved to watch him dunk the ball through the rim.

NBA commissioner David Stern said that Jordan's impact on the league was "tremendous, more than anyone expected." One NBA team's marketing director called him "the Bruce Springsteen of the NBA" because of his tremendous crowd-drawing power. During Jordan's first year in Chicago, attendance at Bulls games almost doubled over the previous season. Ticket sales rose 87 percent from an average of 6,365 fans per game to 11,887. Bulls games even sold out in attendance-poor cities like Oakland and Cleveland. The Bulls were one of seven NBA teams to draw over a million fans in combined home and road games in 1984–85. "I expected a warm reception in Chicago," Jordan said, "but as for those crowds on the road, I can't explain how good it feels to hear those cheers."

Jordan's popularity and his chemistry with fans were displayed even before his first official NBA game. The Chicago rookie was mobbed by screaming teenage girls at an exhibition game in nearby Gary, Indiana. After another exhibition game, a woman who had been unable to obtain Jordan's autograph lay down in front of the car that was carrying him. She refused to move. "I don't care if you run over me," she said, "as long as Michael Jordan is in the car." Police finally moved her.

Jordan's 1985–86 season was curtailed by a broken foot, but the way in which he reacted to the injury again showed his independence and ever-present desire to compete. On October 29, 1985, in only the third game of the regular season, Jordan fractured his left navicular tarsal bone, which supports and stabilizes the ankle and foot. He remained in a walking cast until January 22, 1986, and he did not play again until March 15, 1986.

The Bulls lost 43 of the 64 games they played during the four and one-half months Jordan was out. By mid-March, the Bulls' chance of winning a spot in the play-offs was diminishing. Not only had Jordan been absent, but the Bulls' two best centers had also missed a total of 45 games.

Jordan said of those few months spent in recovery that nothing in his life "comes close to being as depressing." He had lived a seemingly charmed life until that October day in 1985—he had never been seriously injured in high school or college or as a rookie pro.

"Basketball took a lot of my life and I [now] had nothing to spend my time on," Jordan said. "Basketball was a year-round, daily habit with me." When he wanted to resume that habit in March, however, he faced many objections. Bulls' president Jerry Reinsdorf and others felt his return wasn't worth the risk of hurting the foot again.

Jordan was told at a meeting three days before he came back that he risked re-injury and spending four to six months in another recovery effort. The team's general manager, its physician, and two orthopedic specialists also advised against return.

Not worried about re-injury, however, Jordan was determined to play. He had felt ready for nearly a month. Back in Chapel Hill, against doctors' advice, he had started working out again at the University of North Carolina. Jordan's insistence and a discussion with doctors led the Bulls' management to relent and in mid-March, they allowed Jordan to resume play.

After all the conflict, Jordan returned to action in a home game against the Milwaukee Bucks. Bulls' general manager Jerry Krause had instructed coach Albeck not to let Jordan play more than seven minutes in each half. He scored a total of 12 points during the game—accomplished by playing less than six minutes at the end of the second quarter and just under seven minutes at the start of the final period.

Even with Jordan back, the Bulls continued to lose. Jordan was chafing under the 14-minutes-a-game limit to which he had agreed. He urged the team to let him play full time. Jordan got his wish. He began playing for most of the game. In 15 games, he averaged over 20 points a game. He sparked the Bulls to six victories in nine games at the end of the year. A two-point win over Washington, before a crowd of almost 19,000 at Chicago Stadium, clinched a spot for the Bulls in the play-offs.

Entering the play-offs in the spring of 1986 set the stage for Jordan's spectacular, though brief, post-season effort. Jordan put on a brilliant offensive display for fans throughout the country in the second game of a best-of-five series against the Celtics. On April 20, in a nationally televised Sunday afternoon contest, he scored 63 points—an NBA single-game play-off record —breaking Elgin Baylor's record of 61 points, which had stood for 24 years. Despite Jordan's 63 points, the Celtics eventually won the game, 135-131.

A broken bone caused Jordan to miss 64 games in the 1985-86 season, leaving a large void in his daily life.

In the 18 regular-season games in which he played in 1985–86, Jordan made almost 46 percent of his field-goal attempts and 84 percent of his free throws, and he averaged 22.7 points per game. He scored a total of 408 points with 64 rebounds and 53 assists.

In the fall of 1986, Jordan started where he had left off in Boston the previous spring. His foot healed, he scored 50 points in a 108–103 victory in the season opener against the Knicks in New York. In the ninth game of the season, Jordan scored the Bulls' final 18 points in a two-point win over New York at Chicago Stadium, setting an NBA record for consecutive points. In the Bulls' first 20 games, Jordan led the team in scoring with 40 or more points in nine straight games.

"It's nice to have a nuclear weapon on your team," said Doug Collins, who was then the head coach of the Bulls—the third man to fill that spot in Jordan's career with Chicago. Jordan, meanwhile, said modestly that he was not "trying to go out and average as many points as I'm getting. I play the way the team wants me to play. The shots will come either for me or my teammates."

After his explosion in the play-offs the previous spring, Jordan knew other teams would try to tighten their defenses against him. But an expert player like Jordan defies most defensive tactics. After watching Jordan score 40 points against his team, New York

Knicks' coach Hubie Brown said that Jordan "single-handedly beat our traps all night long."

Jordan, "a nuclear weapon"!

The Celtics' Larry Bird said that Jordan was "going to get his points, no matter what." Jordan said of his high point totals, "I like playing the game. I don't treat it as pressure. I don't treat all this scoring as something that's going to happen every day. I know I'm going to have some bad nights, and I'm also going to have some better nights."

He had quite a few of the better nights in 1986–87. Jordan's high scoring didn't stop. He also played in all of Chicago's 82 regular-season games. Jordan's per game average of 37.1 points was 8.1 points better than that of runner-up Dominique Wilkins of Atlanta. During the 1986–87 season, Jordan made 48 percent of his field-goal attempts and almost 86 percent of his free-throw attempts. His 2.88 steals per game was second in the NBA. He also had 430 rebounds, 377 assists, and almost twice as many blocked shots as any other teammate. At a game in Pontiac, Michigan, on March 4, 1987, he scored 61 points.

That game made Jordan the third player in history to score more than 58 points in a game more than once. The other two were Wilt Chamberlain and Elgin Baylor. Five weeks later, on April 16, Jordan again scored 61 points, topping the magical 3,000-point mark. With this second 61-point game of the season he became the only player other than Chamberlain ever to score 50 or more points in three consecutive games. He had scored 50 in Milwaukee on April 13

Wilt Chamberlain, the 7-footer who played in the NBA over 3 decades, holds a host of all-time scoring records including the one for the most consecutive games (7) with 50-or-more points.

and 53 at home against Indiana on April 12.

NBA fans throughout the country loved Jordan. By the 1986–87 season, attendance at Bulls' games averaged almost 16,000, a Chicago Stadium record. In one stretch of 12 home and away games, the Bulls played before 10 sellout crowds.

The Bulls' 1986–87 regular-season record put them in the play-offs. Again, they faced Boston in the first round, and the Celtics won, ending Jordan's third season with the Bulls. After playing only a little more than two full seasons, Jordan was an established star.

Jordan with some of his fans.

5

Sharing His Success

Jordan has traveled a long way from his days as an unpopular teenager. Today, everyone from the youngster on the playground to the corporate executive is attracted to him. His friends say Jordan's easy smile and outgoing manner please people. Off the basketball court, Jordan shows a caring, compassionate, sensitive side of himself. "Certain people have that charisma, full of life and all," coach Collins said. "He's like a magnet. Wherever he goes, he draws people."

One reporter found "a lot of little kid inside that 6-foot, 6-inch body. At times, he seems naive as he wanders about the world." Jordan has often displayed his affection for people, especially children. For example, at a NCAA play-off game in New Orleans in 1982, a streetwise 11-year-old boy talked his way onto the floor during the game and ended up sitting on Jordan's lap. Jordan developed a friendship with the boy, exchanging letters and telephone calls.

While visiting a children's hospital one day, Jordan wrote a check for a donation of $15,000. On Halloween in 1986, the Bulls were playing in New York, so Jordan taped a message on the front door of his townhouse: "Sorry I missed you. If you want trick or treat, come back in three days. Michael Jordan."

Such a considerate gesture is uncommon. Some professional athletes avoid fan contact, and a few even refuse to talk to reporters. Not Jordan—he goes out of his way to answer their questions. Since his first days as a pro, Jordan was a media sensation. As the Bulls moved from city to city in the fall of 1984, the press stalked the rookie. Although some people who knew Jordan said he tired of the same questions, he didn't show it when he was with the news media. He knew that how he answered those questions would make up the image he presented to the public.

Jordan is patient with the media and fans, he says, because "basketball—all my fans—they have given a lot to me. This is my way of giving something back to the community. I'll always remember when I wasn't so popular."

Today, Jordan is extremely popular. His appeal allows him to do product endorsements and promotions, such as television commercials—which can be very lucrative. Jordan employs a Washington, D.C.-

based management group to watch over his financial interests. They carefully screen companies that want to use Jordan to promote their products and try to maintain the former United States Olympic star's all-American image. His major commercial contract is for Nike's Air Jordan line of shoes and clothing.

Despite the intensity level at which the game is played, Jordan exhibits a calm poise on the basketball court.

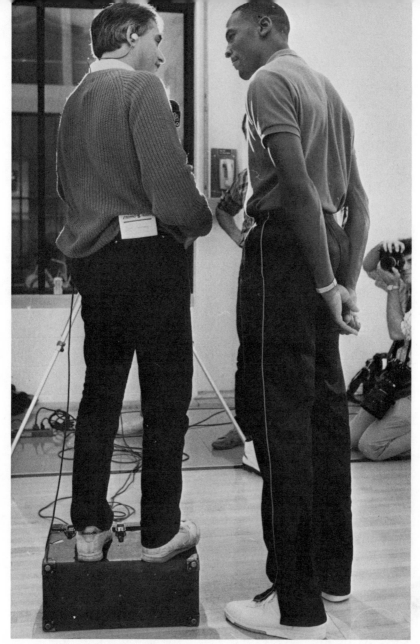

Jordan readily cooperates with the media.

Jordan's seven-year, $6.3 million contract with the Bulls will eventually pay him $1 million a year to play basketball. With his additional income from endorsements, royalties, and appearance fees, Jordan's yearly income is said to be near $2 million.

Jordan's management group also arranges for him to appear at charities and in public service campaigns, which give Jordan additional media exposure. For example, he spent one morning with children afflicted with Down's syndrome while filming an NBA-sponsored commercial for the Special Olympics. Even though he is aware that these appearances contribute to his marketing image, Jordan is dedicated to such activities and genuinely loves children.

Another time, the Bulls were waiting for a late flight at Chicago's O'Hare Airport. A large group of college students recognized Jordan and soon engulfed him, asking for autographs. An airline clerk noticed the commotion and offered to take him to a private office. But Jordan refused the chance to escape and continued to sign autographs and pose for photographs.

In 1986, Jordan's agent, David Falk, said that Jordan—then 23 years old—was "financially set for life." But as Jordan's performance remains strong and his appeal to fans continues to grow, several more years of playing basketball seem to be ahead for him.

In the 1987-1988 season, Jordan was named NBA Most Valuable Player and NBA Defensive Player of

Jordan rises...

...above all competition.

the Year. He played his fifth All-Star game, and he was named the All-Star Game Most Valuable Player.

While the 1987-1988 season was his year for awards, 1989-1990 was Jordan's year for shattering records. He led the league in scoring for the fourth straight year in 1990, and he became the Bulls' all-time point total leader, passing Bob Love's record of 12,623 points. Jordan also scored his career high of 69 points this season, in a 117-113 overtime victory in Cleveland on March 28.

Once again, however, the Detroit Pistons eliminated the Bulls on the way to the championship—for the third year straight. They stopped the Bulls in the Eastern Conference finals, this time in 7 games.

Jordan readily admits that he would love to win an NBA championship. "But if I don't, he says, "I'll walk away with my head held high. I've made a name for myself and earned the respect of my peers, and that can be far greater than any championship."

With or without a championship, Michael Jordan is basketball's favorite celebrity. He draws the crowds to the basketball arena and to their television sets, where he's a favorite guest of "The Arsenio Hall Show" and "Late Night with David Letterman."

Jordan likes expensive clothes and wears Italian suits to business meetings. His overall lifestyle is more practical than wild, however. Chicago Chevrolet dealers had offered him his pick of cars to drive. Instead of a flashy Corvette, Jordan chose a truck because, he said, it would be useful in Chicago's snowstorms.

When the snow stops, Jordan heads for the golf course. He began playing in college, where he became friends with Davis Love III, now on the Professional Golfers' Association Tour. Love gave Jordan his first new set of clubs—with special built-in grips for Jordan's large hands.

Since college, the competitive Jordan has improved his golf game considerably. During the off-season in the summer of 1986, Jordan couldn't run because of the foot he had broken the previous fall. But he could, and did, play golf to stay in shape. Now Jordan tells reporters that he might play professional golf after he quits basketball.

Can he play too much basketball? Jordan doesn't think so—it's a 12–month passion for him. "I don't think I'll ever lose my enthusiasm," he has said. "I love the game of basketball."

MICHAEL JORDAN'S BASKETBALL STATISTICS

University of North Carolina

YEAR	GAMES PLAYED	FIELD GOALS Attempted/Made	%	FREE THROWS Attempted/Made	%
1981-82	34	358/191	.534	108/78	.722
1982-83	36	527/282	.535	167/123	.737
1983-84	31	448/247	.551	145/113	.779
Totals	101	1,333/720	.540	420/314	.748

Chicago Bulls—Regular Season

YEAR	GAMES PLAYED	FIELD GOALS Attempted/Made	%	FREE THROWS Attempted/Made	%
1984-85	82	1,625/837	.515	746/630	.845
1985-86	18	328/150	.457	125/105	.840
1986-87	82	2,279/1,098	.482	972/833	.857
1987-88	82	1,998/1,069	.535	860/723	.841
1988-89	81	1,795/966	.538	793/674	.850
1989-90	82	1,964/1,034	.526	699/593	.848
Totals	427	9,989/5,154	.516	4,195/3,558	.848

NBA Play-offs

YEAR	GAMES PLAYED	FIELD GOALS Attempted/Made	%	FREE THROWS Attempted/Made	%
1984-85	4	78/34	.436	58/48	.828
1985-86	3	95/48	.505	39/34	.872
1986-87	3	84/35	.417	39/35	.897
1987-88	10	260/138	.531	99/86	.869
1988-89	17	390/199	.510	229/183	.799
1989-90	16	426/219	.514	159/133	.836
Totals	53	1,333/673	.505	623/519	.833

1985 Rookie of the Year; NBA All-Rookie Team; Schick Pivotal Player Award
1986 NBA record-holder of most points in playoff game—63—against Boston on April 20, 1986
1987 All-NBA First Team; led NBA in scoring
1988 NBA Most Valuable Player; NBA Defensive Player of the Year; All-NBA First Team; First Team Most Valuable Player; NBA All-Star Game Most Valuable Player; led NBA in scoring; led NBA in steals

REBOUNDS	POINTS	AVERAGE
149	460	13.5
197	721	20.0
163	607	19.6
509	1,788	17.7

REBOUNDS Offensive/Defensive	TOTAL	ASSISTS	PERSONAL FOULS	STEALS	BLOCKED SHOTS	POINTS	AVERAGE
167/367	534	481	285	196	69	2,313	28.2
23/41	64	53	46	37	21	408	22.7
166/264	430	377	237	236	125	3,041	37.1
139/310	449	485	270	259	131	2,868	35.0
149/503	652	650	247	234	65	2,633	32.5
143/422	565	519	241	227	54	2,753	33.6
787/1,907	2,694	2,565	1,326	1,189	465	14,016	32.8

REBOUNDS Offensive/Defensive	TOTAL	ASSISTS	PERSONAL FOULS	STEALS	BLOCKED SHOTS	POINTS	AVERAGE
7/16	23	34	15	11	4	117	29.3
5/14	19	17	13	7	4	131	43.7
7/14	21	18	11	6	7	107	35.7
23/48	71	47	38	24	11	363	36.3
26/93	119	130	65	42	13	591	34.8
24/91	115	109	54	45	14	587	36.7
92/276	368	355	196	135	53	1,896	35.8

1989 All-NBA First Team; NBA All-Defensive First Team; Schick Pivotal Player Award; led NBA in scoring
1990 Bulls' all-time point total leader; led NBA in scoring; led NBA in steals

ACKNOWLEDGEMENTS

The photographs are reproduced through the courtesy of: Christopher Lauber, pp. 1, 9, 12, 14, 47; Jonathan Daniel Photography, pp. 2, 6, 10, 15, 19, 23, 26, 31, 32, 39, 41, 50 (top and bottom), 53, 56; Office of Sports Information, University of North Carolina, p. 20; Chicago Sun-Times, pp. 44, 48; New York Knickerbockers, p. 34; National Basketball Association, p. 43.
Front cover: Christopher Lauber. Back cover: John E. Biever.